Praise for

The Most Overwhelmed Women of the Bible

"Many of my clients, friends, and I wrestle with two common struggles: feeling overwhelmed by our circumstances and emotions and struggling to understand how God meets us in that messy place. Through beautiful storytelling and profound biblical insights from the lives of women in the Bible, Mary DeMuth addresses this dilemma with the truth and grace we desperately need."

—**Ashley Moore**, author, host of the *Heal and Grow* podcast, and Clinical Mental Health graduate student at Liberty University

"Mary writes with raw authenticity, breathing life into these women's stories. In a world where overwhelm is the norm, her words invite us to rediscover peace through Scripture in ways we never expected."

—**Christy Boulware**, author of *Nervous Breakthrough* and founder of Fearless Unite

"Like a skilled artist, Mary DeMuth once again brings biblical women to life through relatable and familiar narratives. She reminds us—too often forgotten—that these figures were real people with real struggles. With her masterful storytelling and timely wisdom, she helps us navigate our own overwhelm, just as these biblical women once did."

—**Stephanie Gilbert**, speaker, podcast co-host, and co-author of *Pastors' Wives Tell All*

"With her typical biblical expertise and warm heart, Mary DeMuth introduces us to the most overwhelmed women in the Bible. I say introduces us because, in many cases, it feels like we are meeting them for the first time with her fresh and riveting descriptions of their narratives. On every page, Mary reminds us all that we have moments of overwhelm and that God remains beside us, no matter what."

—**Chris Morris**, TEDx speaker and author
of *Trekking Toward Tenacity: Your Family's
Roadmap to Stronger Mental Health*

"Mary's rich insight helps us get to know these biblical women as she highlights their struggles, faith, and resilience. This book is a powerful journey with these women and their God that feels deeply personal and relatable. Through Mary's thoughtful writing, she offers her reader hope and an increased desire to lean into God and his Word."

—**Mariel Davenport**, author of *Ruth:
Finding Grace in the Unexpected* and
the TEND Bible study series

"*The Most Overwhelmed Women of the Bible* is beautifully written and profoundly encouraging. It brings fresh insight into the struggles of biblical women and the peace available through God in the midst of overwhelm. With the wisdom and compassion I've come to know Mary for, she brilliantly weaves the stories of biblical women into our own, reminding us that God's presence is steady even when life feels unmanageable. This book is a must-read for anyone seeking biblical encouragement, practical hope, and a deeper trust in God's peace."

—**Monica Ritchie**, host of the *Theologically Fashioned* podcast

"Mary DeMuth's *The Most Overwhelmed Women of the Bible* will captivate the heart of every woman navigating the whelms of life. DeMuth masterfully brings the stories of biblical women to life in a way that allows you to see yourself in their journeys. This book is a reassuring and hope-filled refuge for the overwhelmed heart—a must-read for every woman."

—**Natasha Smith**, author of *Can You Just Sit with Me?: Healthy Grieving for the Losses of Life*

"Mary DeMuth combines incredible storytelling with a biblical narrative flair to give voice to ten of the most overwhelmed women in Scripture. Women everywhere will find themselves within these powerful stories, be reminded they are not alone, and find courage, strength, and sisterhood in the women who have gone before them."

—**Tera Elness**, author of *Sitting with Jesus: A Yearlong Faith Journey*

"In *The Most Overwhelmed Women of the Bible*, author Mary DeMuth vibrantly explores and shares life through the eyes of these Old and New Testament women, allowing us to experience their difficult stories. DeMuth carefully weaves the threads that connect us all in our shared humanity. Rich with history and personality, these chapters give us the hope and peace that an ever-present God comes alongside us too, his precious daughters, in our own overwhelming stress and anxiety—seeing us and loving us."

—**Jodi H. Grubbs**, author of *Live Slowly: A Gentle Invitation to Exhale*

"Mary DeMuth hits it out of the park once more with her book *The Most Overwhelmed Women of the Bible*. She has a unique signature style of bringing the Scriptures to life, making you feel as if you are right there, living the story in real time."

—Dr. Deanna Shrodes, author of *Uncommon Answers: Partnering with the Holy Spirit to Receive Extraordinarily More*

"In *The Most Overwhelmed Women of the Bible,* Mary DeMuth masterfully bridges ancient stories with today's pressures. Her words offer hope and practical wisdom, reminding us that God's presence remains constant even when life feels unmanageable. A gift for every woman who feels she can't catch her breath."

—Rachel Wojo, author of *Desperate Prayers: Embracing the Power of Prayer in Life's Darkest Moments*

The MOST OVERWHELMED WOMEN *of the* BIBLE

The Most Overwhelmed Women of the Bible

How Their Stories Help Us Find Peace

Mary DeMuth

REGNERY
FAITH

Copyright © 2025 by Mary DeMuth

All rights reserved. No part of this book may be reproduced in any manner without the express written consent of the publisher, except in the case of brief excerpts in critical reviews or articles. All inquiries should be addressed to Regnery Faith, 307 West 36th Street, 11th Floor, New York, NY 10018.

Unless otherwise marked, all Scriptures are taken from the Holy Bible, New Living Translation. Copyright © 1996, 2004, 2015 by Tyndale House Foundation. Used by permission of Tyndale House Ministries, Carol Stream, Illinois 60188. All rights reserved.

Scriptures marked NET are taken from the Bible® http://netbible.com copyright ©1996, 2019 used with permission from Biblical Studies Press, L.L.C. All rights reserved.

Scripture quotations marked NASB are taken from the (NASB®) New American Standard Bible®, Copyright © 1960, 1971, 1977, 1995, and 2020 by the Lockman Foundation. Used by permission. All rights reserved. www.lockman.org

Author is represented by Joy Eggerichs Reed of Punchline Agency.

Regnery Faith books may be purchased in bulk at special discounts for sales promotion, corporate gifts, fund-raising, or educational purposes. Special editions can also be created to specifications. For details, contact the Special Sales Department, Regnery Faith, 307 West 36th Street, 11th Floor, New York, NY 10018 or info@skyhorsepublishing.com.

Regnery Faith™ is an imprint of Skyhorse Publishing, Inc.®, a Delaware corporation.

Visit our website at www.regnery.com.

Please follow our publisher Tony Lyons on Instagram @tonylyonsisuncertain.

10 9 8 7 6 5 4 3 2 1

Library of Congress Cataloging-in-Publication Data is available on file.

Cover design by David Ter-Avanesyan
Cover photograph by Courtney Davis

Print ISBN: 978-1-5107-8227-3
eBook ISBN: 978-1-5107-8228-0

Printed in the United States of America

*To the Leakey Family, who have walked
through the valley of overwhelm*

CONTENTS

INTRODUCTION
Overwhelm as Oxygen   xiii

CHAPTER ONE
Sarai, the Disbelieving One   I

CHAPTER TWO
Zipporah, the Nomadic One   23

CHAPTER THREE
Manoah's Wife, the Grieved One   43

CHAPTER FOUR
Naaman's Slave Girl, the Imprisoned One   61

CHAPTER FIVE
Huldah, the Burdened One   75

CHAPTER SIX
Esther, the Fearful One   91

CHAPTER SEVEN
Elizabeth, the Barren One   117

CHAPTER EIGHT
Mary, the Pierced One   135

CHAPTER NINE
The Widow, the Broke One   157

CHAPTER TEN
Priscilla, the Displaced One   173

CONCLUSION
Overwhelmed No More   189

Acknowledgments   191
Notes   193

INTRODUCTION

Overwhelm as Oxygen

I have a tab open on my search bar from my typing, "lost the capacity to relax." I haven't had a chance to peruse the articles, though I want to. And this, even during a supposed vacation where I had some margin. I know I'm not alone. Like you, like every human being on the face of God's beautiful earth, I struggle with being overwhelmed.

Did you know the word's root, *whelm*, is its own word? According to Oxford Languages, whelm comes from *hwelfan* in the Old English, which means to overturn a vessel. So whelm, which used to be in common usage until the late 1800s, has a strong enough meaning on its own. It means to engulf, submerge, bury, flow, or heap up abundantly—particularly at sea.[1] Think of the walls of the Red Sea as they overflowed the once-dry ground to engulf the Egyptian army, or consider Jonah's companions throwing him overboard because of the cacophony of the waves, or perhaps the shipwreck Paul experienced in Malta.

The Most Overwhelmed Women of the Bible

If whelm has such a connotation, *overwhelm* has an even more catastrophic meaning. While it has typically been used as a noun ("My overwhelm is palpable"), today it's more often used as a descriptor ("I feel overwhelmed"). I have friends sputtering through the chaotic waters of overwhelm right now—they lost their ministry; nearly lost one of their children (who died in the mother's arms, then came back to life); lost their reputation; lost a dearly loved parent; and nearly lost their grandchild, who continues to suffer. In a moment of reprieve, another horrific trial whelmed, then overwhelmed them. It has been a privilege to walk alongside them, though I grieve deeply all they have had to endure.

Perhaps you can relate?

As I write this, I am reading through the Bible rapidly—it is a discipline I have practiced over the past several years. When you read the Bible quickly, you begin to see themes arising. And, wow, is there suffering. Beyond the first sparks of creation and the bliss Adam and Eve must have known in the halcyon Garden of Eden, people suffered in a myriad of ways after sin entered the world. At one point, the earth was so wicked and violent that the Lord overwhelmed it with a catastrophic flood. And even when the world dried up, then sprouted life, Noah got drunk, and his nakedness was exposed—even though he was found to be a righteous man.

The longer I live, the more I abhor the so-called "prosperity gospel" that promises if we pull all the right levers, God is obligated to bless us with health, wealth, and social standing. The problem with that way of thinking is the reality of the human condition coupled with the fallenness of our world system. This world cannot satisfy us way down deep; it can only slake our thirst for a moment. It's far more like Edmund's Turkish delight from *The Chronicles of Narnia* series that satisfies for a second but then entices us to want more and more. Once we chase the blessings of God rather than God himself, we tread on an idolatrous treadmill, never quite arriving, but always thinking if we could just get everything right and pull the perfect lever, then we would arrive at our blissful destination. We are overwhelmed with unfulfilled desires, and we are wearing clear out.

The other thing I realized as I read the entirety of the Bible is that the people peopling its pages are real. They are not characters in a play, meant to teach us lessons about life. They worried. They failed. They triumphed. They lost. They questioned. They harmed. They were taken advantage of. They sinned. They had sick days. Like you, they breathed in air, then let it out. And there is much we can learn from them. Some serve as cautionary tales. Others show us the way to live in difficult times. Some reveal the basest of human interactions. Others reveal what genuine love looks like lived out loud.

As a woman, I've become more interested in the female people in the Bible, and I've experienced such joy in unpacking their oft-overlooked stories. As I prayed about this new book, finding overwhelmed ladies was not hard to do. So many of the *Most Misunderstood Women of the Bible* and *The Most Overlooked Women of the Bible* (the first two books in this series) were also overwhelmed.

In this book, like the others, I will flesh out their stories, adding sinew and grit to the existing biblical narrative. I want you to see these women, experiencing life through their eyes. I want you to walk the dusty roads with them, feel their anguish, and find points of connection in their stories. Whenever possible, I quote directly from the NLT Bible, but, to create scenes, I will put my novelist hat atop my historical research mind and add details that make this historical fiction jump off the page—at least that's my intent.

These women faced extreme stress. They were whelmed by life, then overwhelmed. We will examine the stories of these women:

xvi   The Most Overwhelmed Women of the Bible

- Sarai, the disbelieving one
- Zipporah, the nomadic one
- Manoah's wife, the grieved one
- Naaman's slave girl, the imprisoned one
- Huldah, the burdened one
- Esther, the fearful one
- Elizabeth, the barren one
- Mary, the pierced one
- The widow, the broke one
- Priscilla, the displaced one

We see the English iteration of *overwhelm* primarily in the Old Testament. And there, most verses with the idea of being overwhelmed are found in the Book of Job and the Psalms, which makes obvious sense. As noted on Bible Hub, the three primary words for it are:

- *Kasah*, which means to cover over, engulf, or hide
- *Shuph*, which means to break, bruise, or cover
- *Naphal*, which means overthrow, lost, or perish[2]

Overwhelm often deals in water imagery—to be drowned, crushed by waves. Have you ever felt like you were drowning? That no matter what you do, no matter how you flail in life, you can't catch your breath? Wave after wave of trials crash over you, and you're left gasping. Psalm 69:15 speaks to this: "Don't let the floods overwhelm me, or the deep waters swallow me, or the pit of death devour me." In that imagery of waters and drowning, there is a strong connotation of darkness as well. The deeper one sinks into the ocean, the darker it gets. That's why it's beautiful to see how

Kenneth S. Wuest renders John 1:5. "And the light in the darkness is constantly shining. And the darkness did not *overwhelm* it" (emphasis mine).[3]

Friend, if you feel like life is crashing over you, if you're struggling to see your next step in the dark, there is hope. The Lord knows how to rescue those who flail and fear. He loves to care for the straying sheep, the brokenhearted wanderer, and the overwhelmed follower. It's that last phraseology that might trip us up. If we are a follower of Jesus Christ, the true light in all darkness, how is it that we face being overwhelmed? And does it mean we're frail if we feel that way?

We encounter overwhelming circumstances because we live in a fallen world. And it's normal to feel overwhelmed. Even elite apostles felt that way. Paul said it well when he wrote this to the Corinthian church:

> We think you ought to know, dear brothers and sisters, about the trouble we went through in the province of Asia. We were crushed and overwhelmed beyond our ability to endure, and we thought we would never live through it. In fact, we expected to die. But as a result, we stopped relying on ourselves and learned to rely only on God, who raises the dead. And he did rescue us from mortal danger, and he will rescue us again. We have placed our confidence in him, and he will continue to rescue us. (2 Corinthians 1:8–10)

Paul experienced overwhelming circumstances to the point of despairing of life. And in that, God rescued him—but with a lesson. He had to learn and relearn how to stop relying on his own resources and begin to truly find solace and strength in God alone.

xviii The Most Overwhelmed Women of the Bible

Maybe that's where you are in your journey today. You're overwhelmed, yes, but you want to learn all you can in the midst of your current flooded darkness. You want to mine the depths of God's character, searching for him in difficult places. You want to locate him in the rubble. The good news is that he loves to be sought, and as you find him, you will uncover the riches of his love toward you. Paul reflects on this in Romans 8:35–37:

> Can anything ever separate us from Christ's love? Does it mean he no longer loves us if we have trouble or calamity, or are persecuted, or hungry, or destitute, or in danger, or threatened with death? (As the Scriptures say, "For your sake we are killed every day; we are being slaughtered like sheep.") No, despite all these things, overwhelming victory is ours through Christ, who loved us.

You may feel overwhelmed, but victory is yours. You are loved. You are held. You are noticed. You are seen.

May these true stories reorient your heart toward the God who stays with you through overwhelming circumstances. And may you find new aspects of his love as you seek him through your pain. That's my prayer for you.

CHAPTER ONE

Sarai, the Disbelieving One

"I am your princess," Sarai said to Abram, her husband. The fact had been as settled as her name. She was his, and he was hers.

"But princess of where, my dear one?" Abram picked up a stick, then traced the familiar map of their homeland. He drew a star, then poked it with the nib of the branch. "Ur is our home—our former home. And now we find ourselves in Haran as nomads. But for how long?"

Sarai looked at the burial cave where Abram's father, Terah, rested. "I am sorry for our loss, dear Abram. Father brought us here, and now what are we to do? Return to Ur?"

Abram shook his head. "I do not know. Our future is tied with Lot. But I have received no such direction. We must wait."

"Waiting. I do not like waiting much. You know me to be painfully impatient." Sarai knelt before the fire in their camp, stirring the embers. A roasted lamb spiraled above it on a makeshift spit. Cooking in semipermanent spaces was its own worry. But tonight, with the stars nearly singing songs of triumph over her head, she felt in her stomach the worry of anticipation. Living in flux had never been her strength.

She watched as Abram ventured a bit farther from camp, then knelt in the dust. She squinted as the risen moon spotlighted him to the earth. In a moment, he lay prostrate, face kissing the ground, arms akimbo, not moving. YHWH must be talking, she thought. Abram laid that way a long time while birds sang their last songs of the dusk.

When he returned, his face seemed to glow through the visage of dust. "I know what we are to do," he told her. Abram placed his hands on her shoulders and looked into her eyes. The dancing flames of the fire became the perfect backdrop for news of what would be their next adventure. "Sit," he said.

Sarai sat beside him as they watched the fire spark and spit embers into the sky.

Abram pointed heavenward. "The stars," he said.

"Yes, they are beautiful tonight."

He placed a worn hand on her knee. "The Lord said we are to leave Ur completely behind, including all our family and relatives."

"And where will we go?" Sarai's heart thrummed her chest. She would finally know their destiny!

Abram shook his head. "I do not know," he said.

"You do not yet know?"

"No, just that we are to go wherever God leads us."

This was no comfort to her. The stars that had winked in a friendly manner now seemed distant and fickle.

"But there is more to this sojourn," he said. "God made us a promise."

"What good is a promise if I live as a nomad—and without children!" Sarai tried not to raise her voice, but her words came out cracked, high-pitched.

"Would you like to hear what he said?" Abraham sighed, letting out what seemed to be the longest breath.

Sarai nodded. The fire spat and died.

"He said he will make me into a great nation. He will bless me and make me famous, and I will become a blessing to others. He will bless all those who bless me and curse those who treat us with contempt. And then he finished with these words: All the families on earth will be blessed through me."

Sarai said nothing. She had spent her adult life longing for children, but each cycle brought its own cruelty. The Almighty had closed her womb, and it lay dormant. How could he possibly open it at such an age? Still, she trusted Abram, and in the quiet beneath the canopy of stars, as sand gritted her feet, she whispered, "I will go with you."

At seventy-five, Abram possessed uncanny strength. The following morning, he helped break camp as he, his nephew Lot, and everyone in their households left Haran for good. This was no small feat, as they'd acquired many people and livestock. The Lord had further instructed Sarai's husband that they were to move toward Canaan, setting up camp in Shechem. Beside a giant oak tree in Moreh, they encamped, surrounded by Canaanites. This troubled Sarai, and she felt the ambiguity of being out of her element in this new, strange place. It was there that Abram built an altar to the Lord because he had appeared to him again, promising that this very earth they trod would someday be theirs. But right now? They were wayfarers there.

They continued their trek through the hilled country, flanked by Bethel on the west and Ai on the east. Abram, now accustomed

4   The Most Overwhelmed Women of the Bible

to altar-erecting, dedicated another altar to the Lord there. They made their way southward, day by day, toward the Negev. In all of this, Sarai did not complain, though she acquired blistered feet from such a weary march. As famine strangled the land, Abram directed them toward Egypt, which worried Sarai. Would the Egyptians treat them with contempt or favor? Could she trust that Abram's God had their best in mind?

Abram pulled her into an embrace, then whispered in her ear one night as they neared Egypt. "Look, you are a very beautiful woman," he said. "When the Egyptians see you, they will say, 'This is his wife. Let's kill him; then we can have her!' So please tell them you are my sister. Then they will spare my life and treat me well because of their interest in you." Trusting did not come easy to Sarai in this wandering state. Would God spare her if they didn't enact this plan?

She pulled away. This would be a half-truth, she knew. She could not argue with her husband's logic—she actually was his half-sister. Fear told her to be wily in this circumstance, to rely on their cleverness. But she also nursed a greater fear: What would the Egyptians do to her? How would they treat her? Could God be strong enough to rescue her from such a behemoth of a nation?

Under the canopy of palms flanking the mighty Nile River, Pharoah greeted them with pomp. The palatial gardens evoked a feeling of wealth and commerce, and the date trees provided refreshing shade. "You, Sarai, are a princess of great beauty. And a princess like you deserves to live in luxury among us."

Sarai swallowed, shooting a look Abram's way. Surely, he would end this ruse and protect her. She tried to capture his gaze, but he looked to the earth. He gestured for her to follow the palace officials. Her heart sank. How would God protect her? And what of the promised heirs? If she were married off to an Egyptian, what would become of the promise of God? Heart racing, she followed the officials to the Pharoah's harem quarters and prayed. She heard of Pharoah's gifts sent Abram's way—livestock, servants, even camels. And then she waited.

And waited.

Wailing erupted around her as rumors and evidence of plagues broke out among the Egyptians. Pharoah consulted his magicians, who conjured up the reasons for the invasive outbreaks—*it was her!* Pharoah took her to a wide-open courtyard flanking the royal palace, then summoned Abram.

When Sarai saw Abram, she longed to be in his arms. But she stood, waiting, holding back.

Pharoah raised his arms to the skies, then gestured. "What have you done to me?" he shot Abram's way. "Why didn't you tell me she was your wife? Why did you say, 'She is my sister,' and allow me to take her as my wife? Now then, here is your wife." With that, he gently pushed her toward Abram. "Take her and get out of here!" He instructed his men to take them out of Egypt.

And so they sojourned again, the wafting scents of Egypt following them. And Sarai thanked God for protection. She told herself to remember God's faithfulness, promised herself she would believe next time her faith was tested.

They returned to where Abram had erected another altar, near Bethel and Ai, but all was not harmonious as they did so. Lot's shepherds disputed with Abram's, so much so that the situation intensified. It was then that Abram displayed his humility before his nephew, offering him the pick of the land. Sarai asked herself if she would've been so kind. If Lot chose the fertile plains, Abram would take Canaan. Lot selected the beautiful Jordan Valley (*Who wouldn't?* she thought) and settled his family in Sodom, while Abram camped in Hebron near an oak grove in Mamre. As was his custom, Abram built another altar in response to God's clarification of his covenant, a promise from God for offspring and land.

Sarai fretted about Lot's fateful decision as he was carried off from Sodom, then rescued by Abram. God continued to confirm his covenant, asking Abram to drink in the sky, take in the stars, then count them if he could. Those would be the number of their offspring, Abram told her. And, besides her own misgivings and aging body, Abram believed God would keep his promise. They cemented that promise with a late-night ceremony during which God's smoking firepot and flaming torch passed between the carcasses of slain-in-two animals.

But as time is wont to do, it passed slowly, and Sarai's belly never swelled, confirming to her that God would not come through with his promise—at least not in a conventional way. Surely Abram misheard? Or perhaps God needed her help? He could not create a child in her aged womb, this she knew. Ten years in Canaan blossomed her new plan to help God fulfill his promise. She called Abram to her and held his ancient hand. "The Lord has prevented me from having children," she told him.

"But—"

"You know it is the truth. I am far too old. But Hagar—"

Abram shook his head no, but Sarai would not allow a verbal response.

She filled the air between them with instructions. "Go and sleep with my servant. Perhaps I can have children through her." She caught his gaze, while tears streamed down her face. This could be her chance to fulfill God's promise in her own way.

She expected reluctance, which she had discerned in Abram's face before, but he stood, wiped his hands on his tunic, then agreed to her proposal. Initially elated, it didn't take long for her to wonder why he agreed. Did he still want her as his wife? Did he still value her?

Sarai watched as Abram stepped inside Hagar's tent. Her stomach flipped, and she simultaneously prayed for success for her plan and that God would foil it, as well.

But when Hagar's belly swelled with Abram's seed, Hagar, who had been meek and quiet, suddenly found her Egyptian voice, moving from slave girl to a woman of contempt. At every turn, Hagar ridiculed and mocked Sarai, as if boasting her womb were superior to Sarai's. Sarai kept these interactions quiet until everything boiled over like an overfull pot. She called for Abram.

"This is all your fault!" she told Abram.

He shook his head as if to say, *Why?*

"I put my servant into your arms, but now that she's pregnant she treats me with contempt. The Lord will show who's wrong—you or me!"

Abram took her in his arms, then said into her ear, "Look, she is your servant, so deal with her as you see fit." Which then gave her the permission needed to ostracize and condemn the pregnant woman, so much so that the girl ran away.

8 The Most Overwhelmed Women of the Bible

Despite Sarai's satisfaction that she had run off the slave girl, Hagar, head down, returned to camp and gave birth to Abram's firstborn son, a boy whose name meant "God hears"—a gift for Abram's eighty-sixth birthday.

It was after this that God clearly spelled out the conditions of his covenant—once again. He changed Sarai's husband's name from Abram to Abraham, which meant "the father of many nations." And he changed hers from "my princess" to Sarah, which simply meant "princess." She would be the mother of a nation, or so God said. Abraham told her Canaan would eventually be theirs as a possession, though they were foreigners there now. They were to practice a new rite—cutting away the foreskin of all the males in their household, an everlasting sign of the promise of God.

But it was the last detail of Abraham's conversation with the Almighty that perplexed her the most.

Abraham smiled. "God has promised me that you will have a son. You will be the mother of many nations. Even kings will descend from you."

But she would not believe him. How could this possibly happen? Impossible!

The arrival of three unusual men began the day she would never forget. The sun beat down on the visitors that day, and Abraham rushed to her, asking her to bake bread while he prepared a tender calf. Under the shade of the oaks of Mamre, the men talked. One asked, "Where is Sarah, your wife?" She heard this from inside the tent as she leaned toward the voices.

One man said, "I will return to you about this time next year, and your wife, Sarah, will have a son!"

A quiet burst of laughter flew from her before she could rein it in. More like a guffaw than a peal. *How could a worn-out woman like me enjoy such pleasure, especially when my master—my husband—is also so old?*

She heard a reverberating voice, deep as the seas. "Why did Sarah laugh? Why did she say, 'Can an old woman like me have a baby?' Is anything too hard for the Lord? I will return about this time next year, and Sarah will have a son."

She stepped out of the tent, flour meal still upon her hands. "I didn't laugh," she said, hoping she wasn't in trouble.

The response? "No, but you did laugh."

When Sarah returned to the tent, she noticed the men speaking animatedly with words like *destruction* and *Sodom* and *Gomorrah* punctuating their words. All of that was overshadowed by the words of a son. Could it be? Would it be? Was anything too hard for the Lord God Almighty? She knew the correct answer was no—that nothing could stop the way of the Lord. But her heart and emotions, deadened by the years of barrenness, struggled to grasp the possibility. Could she believe such a wonderment?

After the terrifying destruction of Sodom and Gomorrah under the flames of God, they moved again, this time southward toward the Negev to Gerar, where King Abimelech reigned. Though Sarah acquiesced when she played along with Abraham's "she's my sister" ploy, she worried. If this king took her to himself, what would happen to the promise of a son? Thankfully, the Lord yet again rescued her from such a peril, and they continued their wandering. She told herself to remember God's faithfulness and hoped she would not forget his provision.

But one day, the moving, decamping, and reestablishing roiled her stomach. She flushed more beneath the desert heat, and when she had a circle of bread, it erupted through her, and she vomited it upon the earth. This continued to happen. Her monthly flow had long since ceased, so she had very little way of knowing whether this crazy promise of God was coming true—until her belly distended and she began to feel the quickening of feet against her belly. The first time it happened, she laughed, then burst into the tent where Abraham conducted his business.

"What is it, Princess?" he said.

"It happened!"

"What happened?"

"You're going to be a father, Abraham." She pointed to her expanding stomach. "I felt him kick today." Tears flooded her eyes. Decades of unanswered prayers and longings culminated in this moment of impossibility. Unbelievable!

"A child of promise," Abraham finally said. He took Sarah in his arms, his chin resting on the top of her ancient head. "We are indeed blessed. The princess will now have a prince."

Joyful bantering echoed through their home at Kiriath-arba, as Isaac, the embodiment of laughter, was dedicated, grew, and matured beneath the watchful eye of the All Seeing One. Sarah, from *my princess* to *princess*, had the unique and beautiful privilege of raising a son from infancy to manhood. Though God had tested Abraham at Moriah, Isaac remained blessedly alive in the aftermath, a ram providing a substitutionary sacrifice. Though her waiting had cost her years of worry and disbelief, God's promise came to pass in so many ways.

When she was 127 years old, as Isaac celebrated his 37th year of life, Sarah knew her time on the earth drew nigh. Her eyesight dimmed, her breathing grew shallow, and her heart alarmed in her chest, but she thanked God for the surprising privilege of motherhood, something she could never take for granted. She praised him for sustaining her in her geriatric years and giving her supernatural strength to parent such a beautiful child. Though Isaac remained unmarried, she clung to God's promises for his offspring, that from those children the entire world would be blessed.

"Abraham," she called. She lay upon a sleeping mat, the ground biting into her hip bones. She had already said her goodbye to Isaac, though the boy continued to say she would live forever for his sake. She had watched him walk away, lanky and muscular, while weeping followed him out of the tent.

"Princess," Abraham said to her now, tears in his ancient eyes. "I am sorry."

"For what?" She wheezed. "We have had a blessed life, a life of promise fulfilled."

"Yes, but there were two times I endangered you," he said.

She reached toward his face and held his silvered beard in her left hand. "It is forgotten. Please think no more of it."

"I don't want to let you go," Abraham said to the stale air.

Sarah pulled in a ratcheted breath, telling herself not to panic. To need air is to suffocate, she knew. She prayed silently for strength for this unfamiliar journey. God had carried her in his arms thus far; he would not forsake her today on her last moments on earth. "You . . . must . . . let . . . me . . . go."

12 The Most Overwhelmed Women of the Bible

"No," she heard him say as she let out her final breath, praise on her lips.

The Biblical Narrative

We see the story of Sarah throughout the book of Genesis, specifically in chapters 12–18 and 20–23. So much of what she walks through prior to the birth of Isaac is spent in want. To be barren without heirs was considered a curse in ancient days for women, as if God had forsaken them. However, it's important to remember just how many times the Lord reiterated his promise to Sarah's husband, Abraham. Depending on how you categorize each interaction, there are basically nine times God confers with Abraham. But what of Sarah? The only time we see her as a part of that conversation is during the visit of the three mysterious visitors in Genesis 18, and Sarah laughs at the thought of her old, post-menopausal body bearing a son. Many scholars believe that the interaction in that chapter is a theophany, where two angels and God himself visited Abraham's encampment, appearing to mortals in human form. Prior to this, the Lord appeared to Abram in Genesis 12:7–9 to deliver his promise. It's also interesting to note that the three mysterious visitors knew Sarah by name, and Abraham doesn't ask them the question, "How do you know her name?" He must realize that he is talking to One Who Knows.

Considering Abraham's direct interaction with God, Sarah's anguish and waiting takes on more significance. Sarah often had to experience those promises secondhand. Consider waiting decades upon decades for a child in a culture whose only way to create legacy is through childbearing. Imagine the overwhelmed feelings of sadness and despair every single time a period interrupted hope. And then to have her body reverse itself, now unable

Sarai, the Disbelieving One　　13

to carry a child. The overwhelm of such a longing is hard to overstate. And the length of the agony only added to her understandable disbelief.

But Sarah experienced two very frightening situations prior to the promise coming to its miraculous conclusion. First Abram, then Abraham, foisted her onto both Pharoah and King Abimelech where she was supposed to tell both that she was her husband's sister (a quasi-true statement, but it was meant to protect him, not her). In the second occurrence, she must have been in the harem quite some time, because the nation knew that their women were barren because of her presence. You can't instantly perceive the women in your kingdom are barren; it takes many cycles to figure that out. So for two periods of time, Sarai/Sarah was trafficked to keep Abram/Abraham safe. Imagine being sent from the safety of your marriage to live in the home of a powerful leader, where you are meant to be his conquest/wife. Through all of this, we don't hear Sarah's voice. She cannot speak up; she can only trust God to rescue her, which he does. Later, we see her son Isaac do the exact same practice; the apple doesn't fall far from the family tree.

Desperation from the overwhelm of her situation must have also propelled Sarah to make a logical decision that had difficult consequences. Instead of trusting God to do the impossible (and to be fair, there had been little precedent of God ever opening the womb of someone so old), she took the situation into her own hands and gave her servant girl—a slave named Hagar from Egypt—to her husband, a clear violation of the command of God that a man marries only one woman. It's not surprising that once Hagar conceived, Sarah's jealousy, anger, and hatred would arise, along with Hagar's new position as the woman carrying Abram's heir. Conflict inevitably comes after we try to help God make things work out correctly, and we suffer the consequences of our own finagling.

14 The Most Overwhelmed Women of the Bible

Through Sarah's banishment, Hagar leaves once, returns, then leaves finally a second time after Isaac is born. Sarah lives out the rest of her days with Isaac, her promised son, but before he even has offspring. Part of God's covenant with Abraham involved not merely offspring, but land as well. At the closing of Sarah's life, they were still living like sojourners, as foreigners on another nation's soil. No further heirs. No promised acreage.

We see Sarah's faith mentioned in the in the Hall of Faith in Hebrews 11:11–12: "It was by faith that even Sarah was able to have a child, though she was barren and was too old. She believed that God would keep his promise. And so a whole nation came from this one man who was as good as dead—a nation with so many people that, like the stars in the sky and the sand on the seashore, there is no way to count them." Here the author of Hebrews amplifies Sarah's seemingly meager faith amid an impossible situation.

The lesson of Hebrews further emphasizes Sarah's faith by her ability to endure even when not everything God had promised had come to fruition. "All these people died still believing what God had promised them. They did not receive what was promised, but they saw it all from a distance and welcomed it. They agreed that they were foreigners and nomads here on earth" (Hebrews 11:13). We tend to focus only on Sarah's need for a child but forget that the other promise was for a permanent place to call home. She lived the life of a nomad, untethered and wandering. The author of Hebrews praises people like Sarah who "are looking forward to a country they can call their own. If they had longed for the country they came from, they could have gone back. But they were looking for a better place, a heavenly homeland. That is why God is not ashamed to be called their God, for he has prepared a city for them" (Hebrews 11:14–16).

Sarah's life of overwhelm began by leaving everything familiar to her—her home, her family, her life. It continued through the pain of not being able to conceive. She lived through two potentially threatening trafficking situations, then watched as her servant produced an heir without her. All this happened while she moved from place to place, Sodom and Gomorrah were destroyed by fire, and the promises of God seemed more fantasy than any sort of reality.

What Does This Mean for Overwhelmed You?

Transitional Stress

Sarah constantly moved. She did not have the luxury of planning a move; instead, she simply responded to the next sojourn to which God beckoned Abraham. She lived in tents, never permanent homes. She had to be flexible, willing, and resilient.

You may be overwhelmed by transition—by moving from place to place without a solid, permanent home. All of us long for stability. We want to know who our neighbors are. We enjoy the peace that comes from knowing where our favorite grocery store is and how to navigate the streets of our town. When my husband and I and our three kids moved from the suburbs of Dallas to a village above Nice, France, we experienced this kind of displacement. In many ways, we walked Sarah's path—of not knowing the customs or language of the new home we had, of being quite aware of our foreign status, of never getting an inside joke, and constantly making cultural faux pas. Military families experience this often. And our increasingly mobile world means many of us will move from place to place, uprooting and re-rooting.

Author Randy Alcorn has said we were made for a person and a place—the person is Jesus, and the place is heaven.[1] Our longing for roots, stability, and home is simply a yearning for heaven, our true home. This is not a misplaced hope. It's normal, and it's good. But much overwhelm comes our way when we try to retrofit earth with heavenly expectations. No place can ultimately satisfy us perfectly. There is no such thing as greener grass. Though exceptionally hard, the key to experiencing peace in tumultuous moves is twofold: to anchor ourselves to the Rock and learn the art of contentment.

This verse has served me well over the twenty moves I've experienced. King David's words ground me: "He lifted me out of the pit of despair, out of the mud and the mire. He set my feet on solid ground and steadied me as I walked along" (Psalm 40:2). Our semi-permanent state here on earth may fluctuate. Change is its own inevitability. But we are promised permanence in the Unchanging One. James reminds us, "Whatever is good and perfect is a gift coming down to us from God our Father, who created all the lights in the heavens. He never changes or casts a shifting shadow" (James 1:17). Our lives will constantly change, but we can find solace and security in a God who never does. Part of that comes from seeking his permanence when we're living amid impermanence. When I am overwhelmed by constantly changing circumstances, I either give in to that feeling and spiral in my thoughts, or I throw my hands heavenward and ask God to please help me find perspective.

And in that surrender, life becomes a treasure hunt for his permanence and goodness. That's probably why Paul reminds us that seeking contentment is work. It involves action and pursuit. It must be learned. He writes, "Not that I was ever in need, for I have learned how to be content with whatever I have. I know how to live on almost nothing or with everything. I have learned the secret of living in every situation, whether it is with a full stomach or empty, with plenty or little. For I can do everything through Christ, who gives me strength" (Philippians 4:11–13). We often pluck the latter verse from its important context. Doing "everything" involves learning contentment in *every* circumstance—when we're experiencing abundance and when we're walking through lack, when we're settled in or we're constantly moving from place to place, like Sarah did.

Infertility

Sarah walked through decades of a closed womb, though she was promised a child. Because Abram could conceive with Hagar, it can be logically deduced (though not proven) that Sarah could not carry a child for whatever biological reason. We could argue that this long-standing inability was part of God's glorious plan for a miracle, but Sarah did not know any of that during her long sojourn of waiting. There were no medical tests back then, no ultrasound equipment, no way of knowing the why of her infertility struggle. She simply could not bear a child, and this not only would have meant shame for her in a culture that provided for a family's lineage through its male offspring, but also a stigma. Beyond how that pain would interact with her culture and family, it's probable that she suffered deep sadness and frustration. Perhaps she wrestled with God, wondering why he wouldn't grant her request. And she most certainly struggled to believe that God could do such an impossibility.

The longing for children, though not universal, is a deep wound if it's not fulfilled. It reminds me of a friend of mine who longs to be married but continues to remain single—against her desire. She prays often. I pray, too. But so far there are no prospects in her life. She has often asked the Lord why. She has wept. She has questioned God's goodness. She tries very hard to be content alone, but the years are wearing on her. The question becomes: Does God love me? I would imagine that Sarah wondered that, too.

Unfortunately, this life is not a formula, and God is not a genie who grants our every wish. He is sovereign with a plan that's often

18   The Most Overwhelmed Women of the Bible

unknowable in the moment. It's only later, when we look back on things, that we see God's wisdom in not granting us what we wanted. My friend Sandi longed to have a child. They tried so many avenues, including failed adoptions, before eventually adopting a little girl. That angst and pain brought her to seminary, then a doctoral program where she eventually studied this verse: "But women will be saved through childbearing, assuming they continue to live in faith, love, holiness, and modesty" (1 Timothy 2:15). She wrote the book *Nobody's Mother: Artemis of the Ephesians in Antiquity and the New Testament*, which brings scholarship and nuance to the question of whether having children is salvific. Had she not experienced the weight of infertility, she most likely would not have explored this scholarship, which added to a longstanding debate with nuance and intelligence.

Unanswered Prayer

Sarah's infertility represented a decades-long unanswered prayer and likely a yearslong wrestling with belief. Perhaps you haven't struggled with infertility, but you have this one prayer request that seems to be rote, repetitive, and unheard. Does God care? Does he hear? Can he be believed? No matter how you ask, and even when you grow tired of making the request, the answer remains no. This seeming lack of movement is its own overwhelm and threatens our trust muscle. We may ask why the Lord doesn't seem to be as concerned about our worry or longing as we are. We may be overwhelmed by our current circumstances that don't seem to be changing.

I had a prayer I'd been praying for four decades for a loved one to become a Christ-follower. I prayed often in the beginning. I worried I had not done "enough" for that person to see Jesus in me. I wrote out my prayers, wept my prayers, and questioned my prayers. Did they even matter? Was God listening? Did he care about her as much as I did? There were many times I wondered if prayer *worked*. Eventually, I had to make peace with the fact that the other person had a free will, and I could not make her follow Jesus. Nor could I guarantee that God would save her. This was its own grief and caused a lot of sadness. I came to the place where I had to make peace with all I had done, surrendering her to God's capable hands. As I mentioned earlier, this echoed what the saints in Hebrews 11 experienced. They longed for something but didn't always receive what they were longing for—at least in this life.

This is a hard truth, a haggard hallelujah, a deep disappointment—all of which exacerbate our feelings of overwhelm. God doesn't always answer our prayer the way we want him to. And even if he does, he sometimes does so in a surprising way (a ninety-year-old having a baby, for instance). So how are we to live in light of this? How are we to find joy when a prayer remains unanswered? We must find solace in God himself—even more than his answers. Jesus did this as he pulled away from the crowds to spend time with his Heavenly Father. Before he could face the demands of constant ministry, he needed to be poured into. He needed the permanence of the Father's love to compel and propel him.

In an article I wrote for Logos Bible Software, I unpacked the famous verse about delighting in the Lord (Psalm 37:4). To delight means to take pleasure in, to find joy alongside. I wrote,

> Similarly, when we can't wait to spend time with God, when we experience his amazingness, it's because we love how he treats us. And his love for us causes us to love others. We learn best by experience, and we cannot demonstrate what we first haven't walked through. Perhaps

this is why Jesus had such strong words for those who appeared righteous on the outside but were something else altogether on the inside. Their heart and their actions did not match. But when we spend time delighting in God, he changes our insides so that our good actions flow naturally from a changed heart.[2]

To shift from depending upon answered prayers for our joy to taking great delight in the One who created us causes a change in perspective. It's like the difference in my adult child feigning love for me in order that I would give them money versus my adult child simply spending time with me because they love me. The first is a transactional relationship; the latter is a loving one.

Perhaps you have battled disappointment over an unanswered prayer because you've grown guilty of expecting God to grant your every wish. Sometimes we wrongly believe that God's love only means him answering prayers according to our desire and timing. We have looked to God as the granter of desire rather than simply desiring God.

Unfulfilled Timing

Perhaps our overwhelm doesn't specifically stem from an unanswered prayer per se, but from the timing of that answer. Imagine the years Sarah's longing went unsatisfied, how they must have dragged on, so much so that when she heard the promise out loud, her response was to laugh in disbelief. How ridiculous it all must've sounded, particularly as an eighty-nine-year-old! Sarah's longing did get fulfilled, yes, but certainly not in the timing she would've wanted it to. And that's often when our overwhelm grows.

It's interesting to note that God reminded the exiled Israelites in Isaiah 43:18–20 to do two things—to remember how he answered their longings in the past, but to then forget all of it. Why? Because God declared, "For I am about to do something new. See, I have already begun! Do you not see it?" (Isaiah 43:19a). God was going to bring the nation from the bowels of exile back to Jerusalem. The wall surrounding the city would be built in record time, and they would, as a remnant, have a home and a place of worship. This would be done supernaturally and not through conquest. When we are overwhelmed, our grip on control tightens, and our prayers tend to get very specific. We want the Lord to answer those prayers in the way we prescribe them. But although we are to remember the beautiful faithfulness of God and how he answered our prayers in the past, we must leave room for our creative God to be creative in his answers. He will do something new, unexpected, which makes our walk with him even more interesting.

God's timing is not our own, and when we base our happiness on our preconceived expectations of how God is supposed to answer our prayers, we will most likely be disappointed. There is great relief in opening our hands and hearts and telling the Lord, "I don't know how you will answer this longing, but I trust you to work in a way that brings you glory. Help me to be patient while waiting for your unique plan to unfold. Fill me up with belief!"

Sarah did receive her promise. God was utterly trustworthy and powerful in the way he brought about his plan. But in the in-between time, Sarah faltered (as all of us do). She resorted to logic (giving Abram her servant girl). She doubted. She harmed another (Hagar). Like Sarah, we are waiting on God to answer our prayers. But despite God's seeming delay in answering, his goodness toward us is not dependent on our perfect faith. When we are overwhelmed, and that overwhelm causes us to disbelieve, God still loves us and is unfolding his plan before us.

Truths About Faith-Filled You

- Even when it seems like God is not working, he is working behind the scenes to answer your prayers.
- Our human frailty does not negate God's goodness.
- God watches out for us even when others have placed us in difficult or scary situations. He sees us. He defends us.
- Unmet expectations do not mean God has forgotten us.
- God loves to do something new.

Questions for Discussion

1. What did you initially believe about Sarai (Sarah) before you picked up this book?
2. How does your life mirror Sarah's? How is it different?
3. What do you admire about Sarah?
4. In what ways is Sarah's story a cautionary tale? What does her life teach you about what *not* to do?
5. What changes have taken place in our world since Sarah's battle with infertility? How has her struggle remained the same for women today?

CHAPTER TWO

Zipporah, the Nomadic One

The man certainly didn't look familiar. Zipporah whispered to one of her sisters that he looked like an Egyptian. His face spoke volumes, she could see, as if each crease carried the weight of a too-heavy burden. But whatever heaviness settled in on his soul, he did not allow it to change his kindhearted manner. Some let pain ruin them toward bitterness and suspicion, but others allowed their pain to tame their anger. He was the latter, she knew.

Midian had its own traps and dangers, especially when watering time loomed in the heat of the day. Though the daughters of Reuel, also known as Jethro, were seven in number, the hulking weight of the other shepherds often intimidated them. Zipporah had steadied herself, taking deep breaths to calm the heart that often beat faster at the sight of the thugs hovering over the well.

But this day felt different. The air was charged, buzzing between the Egyptian and the gathering group of men who were already shooing Zipporah's sheep from the well's wide opening.

The Most Overwhelmed Women of the Bible

They acknowledged the foreign man, but his presence did little to stop them from heaping disdain upon her sisters and kicking their flock toward the wide-open expanse. It was as if his quiet presence made them even more daring, as if their bullying felt more exciting with an audience. Dust swirled up beneath their shouting kicks.

Zipporah licked dry lips, then swallowed. This would not end well. The men would, once again, scare away their timid sheep, pull up the water nearer the surface, and force them to come at the day's hottest point to retrieve water much deeper down. It exhausted her, but it was her lot as one of seven daughters of a priest in the wilds of Midian.

The man who had been seated at the well's mouth stood to his full stature. He did not raise his voice, but he resonated with authority. "Leave," he said. One word. Initially, the men mocked such a request, but the Egyptian said nothing more and just stared at each shepherd without breaking his gaze.

One by one, the men left.

Zipporah let out the breath she'd been holding in. Now she could rally her sisters to gather the sheep and water them until they were satisfied. She could fill their heavy water carriers to the brim to water the rest of the flock at home.

But that is not what happened.

"Allow me," the Egyptian said. He pointed to the sisters' water carriers and filled each one, not mentioning why and certainly not expecting a thank you. It was as if his kindness was its own reward. He helped regather the straggling sheep and gently encouraged them to drink their fill. And then he sent them all on their way, saying nothing more. He sat again at the well's edge, quiet.

Zipporah worried a bit for him. Would those scoundrels return with more men to pay him back for their humiliation?

Zipporah, the Nomadic One

Once back at their homestead, Father rushed to greet them.

"Zipporah, why are you back so soon today?" His eyebrows raised in a question.

She took his hands in hers, marveling at their roughness. "An Egyptian rescued us from the shepherds," she said. "And then he drew water for us and watered our flocks." She followed Father to his main tent.

He turned toward her. "Then where is he?"

For a moment she couldn't respond, because wasn't the answer obvious?

"Why did you leave him there?" he asked.

Zipporah shook her head. She suddenly felt bad for not rewarding the mysterious man with an offer of hospitality. He had seemed forlorn and forsaken there beside the well.

"Invite him to come and eat with us." Father pointed in the direction of the well. His voice had not been harsh, more like teasing. He had always been a wise priest, a man who loved to love others. Unlike the shepherds who harmed sheep and women alike, he was a kind man full of insight into human nature. And he had a heart for hospitality, viewing it as a privilege. How many times had he said those very words to Zipporah?

She traveled with one of her sisters back to the well as the sun dipped low, scattering pinks and purples near the horizon line. When she saw the man sitting in the same place she had left him, she pulled the veil tighter over her face. "My father would like to extend kindness your way. Would you come to our home for provisions and shelter?"

The man nodded and said no words until they reached home.

Father greeted him with a kiss on each cheek. "Thank you for taking care of my daughters," he said. "I am Reuel. I am a priest here, and I am grateful for you, Egyptian."

26 The Most Overwhelmed Women of the Bible

"I am Moses," the man said. "I am not an Egyptian." He took a long drink of wine.

Father nodded. "What is your heritage, then?"

"I am an Israelite, though I was adopted by a Pharoah. It is because of that adoption and the defense of my countrymen that I am here."

"So we are brothers," Father said. "Through Abraham's lineage, through his wife Keturah."

Suddenly, the familiarity of Moses made sense to Zipporah. Though he dressed as an Egyptian, his kindness reminded her of her own father.

They spoke well into the night, and as the insects rested under a full moon, Father invited Moses to stay with them to work and protect them all. Perhaps he would accompany her and her sisters tomorrow and deliver them from the shepherds again.

<hr/>

Zipporah thanked the God of All for the privilege of marrying Moses, the man of God, the one who had rescued her months ago. From time to time, Moses would regale her about his time spent in Pharaoh's house, his deep longing to see his family, and his fear that if he returned, he would be executed.

"Perhaps not," she said one evening, her belly swollen from pregnancy.

"I am a murderer. I killed an Egyptian. The penalty is clear." He looked through the doorway of their tent that always faced home to him. Tears formed in the corners of his aging eyes.

Zipporah wanted to wipe them away, wanted to stave off the loneliness and isolation seemingly imprinted in the fabric of her husband, but some wounds were too raw to be salved. As his tears flowed silently, a rush of water flew from her while her belly cramped. "Go and fetch the midwife," she said.

The pangs of childbirth upon her, Zipporah gripped the hand of the midwife's helper as she panted through waves of pain. She told herself to remember there would be a reward at the end of all this labor.

"It is time," the midwife said. "Look at me. Look me in the eyes."

Zipporah obeyed, though she stifled a low growl.

"Now push!"

With a loud cry, Zipporah contracted her abdomen, then heard the blessed cry of a little one.

"A boy," the midwife said.

When Moses entered the tent and held his firstborn son, Zipporah wondered what name he would give him. Would his name mean strong? Intelligent? A servant?

"Gershom," Moses finally said.

Zipporah nodded. Her husband's choice made perfect sense. Of course he would choose a name that mimicked his longing. It meant, "I have been a foreigner in a foreign land." No matter how she tried to convince Moses that he had a new, established life here in Midian, he could not and would not let his heart settle there. And now their son carried his anguish.

When their second son roared his way into the world, Zipporah wondered if now, perhaps, her husband felt more settled in her homeland. But he named the boy Eliezer, which she knew to mean "help of my God."

"Why that name?" she asked.

28 The Most Overwhelmed Women of the Bible

Moses stroked the brow of the newborn. He looked at her as if the answer were obvious.

"I really don't understand." She took the boy from Moses, then cradled him in her arms.

"The God of my ancestors was my helper."

"Yes," she said. "And he helped you to find us here in Midian."

He turned away. "No, that's not what I meant. God rescued me from the sword of Pharaoh."

Zipporah nodded. Always pondering his past, her husband's heart had been tethered always to Egypt and the plight of his people like an unwavering pull. It was then she knew, as if God had confirmed it entirely, that he would one day return to his people—and take her with him.

Not long after, Moses returned from tending her father's flock near Sinai, God's mountain. Moses's face had a different countenance to it, as if God himself had erased some of his wrinkles and restored vitality to his eyes. "I have heard a message from God," he told her.

"And what did he look like?"

"I did not see him, but I heard him from a bush that burned hot but was not consumed. His voice came from that mysterious shrub. He told me to take off my sandals because I was standing on holy ground."

"Did you?" Zipporah paced the tent. This could only mean that everything she knew to be familiar would be upended.

"Of course. I could not even look that way. I was afraid. Even so, the Lord spoke to me, telling me he had seen the oppression of the Israelites, my people, and that he has heard their cries of distress."

Zipporah, the Nomadic One

"And he is sending you as deliverer," she said, letting out a breath. She paced.

"Yes, but who am I? I am old. I am slow of speech—you know that."

She said nothing.

"And another thing." Moses stood and paced their tent. "God told me his name. I AM WHO I AM."

Zipporah shuddered. Light and dread and fear and joy flooded through her all at once. The One who made the stars, their sheepfold, all human beings, had spoken to her husband, had specifically called him. She would not stand in I AM's way.

"God told me to tell the elders of Israel, 'Yahweh, the God of your ancestors—the God of Abraham, Isaac, and Jacob'—has appeared to me. I am to tell them that the Lord has heard their cries, and that he will lead them all away from the oppression of Egypt toward what he calls a Promised Land—what he had promised our Father Abraham under a canopy of stars."

"And what did God say would happen after that?" She dipped a drinking ladle into their water pot and drank. Fear niggled at her roiling stomach.

"He said Pharoah would be stubborn after I asked him to let us go worship Yahweh after a three-day journey into the wilderness. He said eventually Pharoah will let us go, and we will leave with gifts from the Egyptians." Moses told her of a staff that would turn into a snake and leprosy that would appear and disappear. And that his brother Aaron would become his mouthpiece.

"There is only one thing you need to do," she said, letting out a long sigh. "Ask my father for his blessing and permission."

Moses immediately approached her father, Reuel. After explaining his encounter with God on Mount Sinai, he said, "Please let me return to my relatives in Egypt. I don't even know if they are still alive."

"Go in peace," Father said. He blessed them all, shedding tears.

Zipporah mounted a donkey, along with their two sons. Moses walked ahead of them, carrying the staff of God. She turned back to see Father disappear into the horizon as they headed toward an unknown fate. The smaller he got, the more fearful she became. Father had been her steady constant, her rock, the wisest man she had ever known. His prayers would follow them, but would she ever see him again?

That evening, a swirl of holiness and vengeance engulfed their temporary camp. Zipporah awakened to what could only be described as Death personified, readied to kill Moses. She did not have time to process what was happening while the booming voice caused her to tremble. At once she knew the cause—one son had lived uncircumcised until this sacred, scary moment. Zipporah dug around their belongings until she found the knife made of flint. She pulled away his tunic, exposing him naked to the cool night air. He looked at her, a dreadful question in his eyes.

She prayed.

He began to cry now.

She took the knife, reminding herself that doing the act quickly would save him more pain. In a flash of a moment, she circumcised their son. Blood dripped from her hands while her boy let out a blood-clotting scream. Before wrapping him back up, she took the foreskin and placed it at her husband's feet. In tears, she said, "Now you are a bridegroom of blood to me."

In the only way a storm can rage then suddenly dissipate, the holy wrath of God's vengeance upon her husband vanished, as if it had never been there like warm sunshine after a wailing torrent.

She wrapped her son tightly in an embrace, singing the songs of her father over the tear-stained boy. Her tears mingled with his, so she wiped away them all from his ruddy cheeks.

Even though all was well, Zipporah's heart pounded like a drumbeat the rest of the night. She knew they faced much, much more when they neared the mighty Nile's shores. But at least God would be fighting on their behalf, not against them as he had been that terrifying night of small-scale bloodshed.

Zipporah treasured the miraculous in her heart. In a very real way, she and Moses's two sons endured the plagues and trials brought on by Pharoah's hardened heart together. But before the nation's victorious march through the bowels of the Sea of Reeds, before the songs of triumph when God covered their enemy in a watery grave, before the complaining in the wilderness, Moses sent her back to Midian. His words came suddenly, without provocation, but they were resolute, as if he had made the decision then engraved it in stone. It would be for their protection, he had said. She and their sons were not to venture on with them. No, they must return to Midian now, back to Father's protective house. How long they would be separated could not be known or discerned. So, with heaviness, she reversed her previous journey and mounted a donkey, only this time it was the figure of her husband that faded into the horizon behind her.

Zipporah's heart quickened when Father said it was time to see Moses, particularly since the Israelites been delivered from Egypt with such strength. The rumors of God's power allowed for good storytelling with her sons, though their constant asking about Moses broke her heart.

But now!

They would see their father.

They ventured northward through the desert, again on the back of donkeys, toward Canaan and through a long wilderness. Once they arrived at the encampment, Father sent a message to Moses. He wrote, "I, Jethro, your father-in-law, am coming to see you with your wife and two sons." He rolled up the papyrus and sent it with a messenger who knew where Moses stationed himself.

"He has called for me, dear Zipporah," Father told her. "I will go out and meet him, then send for you."

Father told her of their meeting, how Moses honored him by bowing to the earth and kissing him. After Moses recounted the nation's trials and triumphs, Father had proclaimed what Zipporah already knew about him. "Praise the Lord," he had said, "for he has rescued you from the Egyptians and from Pharoah. Yes, he has rescued Israel from the powerful hand of Egypt! I know now that the Lord is greater than all other gods, because he rescued his people from the oppression of the proud Egyptians."

"What did you do next?" Zipporah looked out from their tent, then back at her sons, longing filling her heart.

"We offered burnt offerings and sacrifices to God. And then we ate a meal together."

Zipporah wanted to ask why Moses had not sent for her or their sons, but she kept quiet. He who rescued her from angry shepherds was himself a shepherd of many multitudes now. He must have been consumed with the responsibility, at least according to Father's rendition of Moses's overwhelming duties to a hostile, ungrateful nation. Still, she ached inside, wondering if this loneliness would befall her for the rest of her days. Would they have quiet moments to talk as they did in the days of Midian?

When Father left for home, her feelings of isolation grew.

Zipporah did understand Moses more, though. Living in a foreign land with little or no points of common reference, she felt out of sorts, overwhelmed by the needs of the people around her, and bone-wearied from the constant moving behind cloud and fire. Her longing to return to her people, what was known to her, ached in her heart. And yet? She knew God had made way for a mighty deliverance—a supernatural freeing that could only be described as miraculous. To be God's chosen people on a journey toward a new land—this settled her when she felt overcome with longing for Father and their home in Midian. There would be a new, permanent home, flowing with milk and honey, free of pestilence and war. That is what she prayed as she watched the sun sink low into the curve of the horizon.

The Biblical Narrative

A lot of important things happen at wells throughout the Bible, but in the earliest passages, we see matrimony to a deliverer. In Genesis 24, we experienced the wife of Isaac (Rebekah) being selected by Abraham's servant at a well—and she is watering sheep. Later, in Genesis 29, Jacob rolls away the stone for Rachel, who becomes his wife alongside Leah. That family inevitably makes up the twelve tribes of Israel. And here we see the meeting of Moses and his wife, Zipporah. In this occurrence, we see an exiled Moses who failed to deliver his people (through murder) beginning to learn God's lessons about deliverance. In one small act, he whose name means "the drawing out of water" rescues Reuel's shepherdess daughters. It's the beginning of forty years of lessons the Lord would have for him.

Zipporah must have known Moses's longing for his family and people, particularly through the names he gave their children. In fact, the word used for "drove away" in the well scene, *garash*, is a nod toward Gershom. Moses fled from Pharoah, and according to his second son's name, he escaped the sword of Pharoah through God's supernatural hand. Though it's impossible to truly know because the text is silent on this issue, there's a strong probability that Moses had residual trauma from his time under Pharoah's roof, experiencing the sting of adoption, particularly when so many boys had been murdered by his "father," and yet he remained alive. Not to mention the circumstances surrounding Moses's failed attempt to deliver his nation through violence.

Zipporah's name means "bird" and comes from the verb *sapar*.[1] Though we don't know from the text how this nomenclature correlates to her personality, it is interesting to remember all the beautiful ways God includes birds in the Bible. A bird revealed when it was time to leave the ark in Noah's day (see Genesis 8:7). God confirmed his covenant with Abraham as he walked through the middle of a bird carcass (see Genesis 15:10). Moving to the New Testament, not one bird falls to the ground without the Father's notice (see Matthew 10:29–31). They don't sow or reap, but God provides for them (see Luke 12:24). God cares for his creatures, and he cared for Zipporah, giving her a husband and two sons.

And he used Zipporah to deliver Moses. Though it is not stated that she studied the ways of God, the Abrahamic covenant was sacred to her. And if Moses was to be a deliverer to the people of the covenant, he would have to practice the tenets of that covenant. In Genesis 17:9–14, we see the preciseness and necessity of this covenantal practice:

Then God said to Abraham, "Your responsibility is to obey the terms of the covenant. You and all your descendants have this continual responsibility. This is the covenant that you and your descendants must keep: Each male among you must be circumcised. You must cut off the flesh of your foreskin as a sign of the covenant between me and you. From generation to generation, every male child must be circumcised on the eighth day after his birth. This applies not only to members of your family but also to the servants born in your household and the foreign-born servants whom you have purchased. All must be circumcised. Your bodies will bear the mark of my everlasting covenant. Any male who fails to be circumcised will be cut off from the covenant family for breaking the covenant."

When Zipporah understood that God would take Moses's life for his failure to circumcise their son, she did it herself. (It is interesting to note that he was supposed to be circumcised on the eighth day, but he was mostly likely significantly older than this when she cut his foreskin). In the narrative, I did not delineate which son she circumcised because it is not mentioned in the text.

In some ways, her act is a foreshadowing of what would happen in the Passover. Blood would be shed, then smeared over doorposts. An angel of death (who could also be what Zipporah encountered) would kill firstborns for whom there was no blood as a covering. In this case, their son's blood caused God to pass over Moses. He relented in taking his life. And now because of Zipporah's quick action, Moses would be the deliverer God would use to free an entire nation.

What Does This Mean for Overwhelmed You?

Following Another's Dream

Zipporah, like Sarah, would've encountered culture shock and transitional stress when she ventured with Moses to Egypt, back to Midian, then to the borderlands of Canaan after the exodus. Her overwhelm may have resulted from the pain of following another person's dream rather than her own. She was not intended to be Israel's deliverer, but her marriage to Moses meant that his obedience would cost her. It reminds me of a favorite quote of Oswald Chambers:

> If we obey God it is going to cost other people more than it costs us, and that is where the sting comes in. . . . We can disobey God if we choose, and it will bring immediate relief to the situation, but we shall be a grief to our Lord. Whereas if we obey God, He will look after those who have been pressed into the consequences of our obedience. We have simply to obey and to leave all consequences with Him.[2]

This is a hard lesson for both parties. Sometimes our obedience to the things of God causes pain for others. This happened to my family when my husband, Patrick, and I moved overseas to France to plant a church. It cost us, yes, but it also cost our children. And sometimes our spouse's (or friend's, or parent's, or relative's) obedience will cost us. And therein lies the overwhelm.

Navigating the Grief and Pain of Another

Sometimes our overwhelm does not simply erupt from our own circumstances. Sometimes it emerges from something we cannot control: the grief and pain of another. There have been times in our own marriage where I have been crushed by the pain my husband has experienced, or when I felt powerless to help him work through particular issues. It can be isolating and lonely when one spouse struggles. I imagine Zipporah bore some of the weight of Moses's pain—of feeling like an outcast, afraid, and like a fish out of water. In times like this, it's important to remember to carry those burdens, but not fully. Jumping forward to the New Testament, the Apostle Paul has some wise words for us all in Galatians 6:2–5:

> Share each other's burdens, and in this way obey the law of Christ. If you think you are too important to help someone, you are only fooling yourself. You are not that important. Pay careful attention to your own work, for then you will get the satisfaction of a job well done, and you won't need to compare yourself to anyone else. For we are each responsible for our own conduct.

We are to share and bear the burdens of others, but not so much that we take away someone's personal responsibility. We, according to verse five, are responsible for our own conduct.

Thankfully, Jesus reminds us that he loves to bear our burdens and give us a lighter load (see Matthew 11:28–30). We are not responsible for fixing another's problems (that is far too much of a weight to bear). We are responsible for ourselves alone. Yes, we can love, pray for, and give wise counsel. We can serve and listen. But we must first give the Lord the burden of bearing the weight of another's sorrow. That's when rest overwhelms our overwhelm.

Dealing with a One-Sided Relationship

Although the text does not explicitly say that Moses neglected Zipporah (perhaps he sent her back to Midian to protect her and their children from an unknown future), there is evidence that he did not interact with her once she ventured to Canaan with her father. He did not call to meet with her when Jethro specifically told him that his wife and sons were with him. He told the nation to not have sexual intercourse prior to meeting with God (See Exodus 19:2), so it's likely that even after Zipporah returned to him, they did not consummate, at least for a while. After that, she is not mentioned again. It's only later in Numbers 12:1, when Miriam and Aaron speak against Moses for marrying a Cushite woman, that we see the possibility of Moses having a second wife. (Whether Zipporah died or was alive at the time of this marriage is unknown.) He did not have offspring with this second wife, but the question remains—what happened to Zipporah?

Many who are in neglected, broken, or ambivalent marriages feel a large amount of overwhelm. Why? Because unless the other returns to them, there is little that can be done to win a spouse back. We are only responsible for our side of things. Paul reminds us that we can "do all that you can to live in peace with everyone" (Romans 12:18). But we cannot do another's work for them. We cannot change the heart of another. We cannot make someone love us. We cannot repent on behalf of another. In that, there can be a lot of waiting for God to change the situation. But sometimes he does not. And that's where the pain enters in. To be overwhelmed in marriage is its own personal Gehenna. The act of surrender is your only solace. You can ask the Lord what he wants you to do, then do it. But you cannot fix a broken marriage on your own. Yet you can rest in knowing that the Lord truly understands what it's like to be in that kind of relationship because he often used marital imagery in talking about his relationship with the nation of Israel.

Consider this plea by the Lord through the prophet Isaiah:

> "For your Creator will be your husband; the LORD of Heaven's Armies is his name! He is your Redeemer, the Holy One of Israel, the God of all the earth. For the LORD has called you back from your grief—as though you were a young wife abandoned by her husband," says your God. "For a brief moment I abandoned you, but with great compassion I will take you back. In a burst of anger I turned my face away for a little while. But with everlasting love I will have compassion on you," says the LORD, your Redeemer. (Isaiah 54:5–8)

Israel was unfaithful to the Lord. They chased after idols and unspeakable acts of worship toward foreign gods. The Lord often warned them not to play the prostitute with the gods of the surrounding nations, but they would not heed his counsel. Though the Lord loved Israel, he loved them enough to allow their sinful choices to exile them for seventy years. Allowing someone to experience their own fallout is an excruciating thing to walk through.

Feeling the Sting of Unseen-ness

There is also the overwhelm that comes from being unseen. Whether Zipporah was supplanted by a second wife, or she simply died in obscurity, or she was given a new name as Moses's wife (yet another possibility), she is no longer heard of during the remainder of Israel's wanderings. Have you ever felt that way? Here we have a wife who saved a savior from being killed.

The Most Overwhelmed Women of the Bible

Had she not acted quickly and decisively, Moses would not have been God's deliverer for the nation. And yet, it seems her role diminished over the years. Those who age (all of us!) feel this in our gut. We used to live in the overwhelm of spiritual work and activity only to be supplanted by aging out of usefulness. No longer busied with task upon task or prayer upon prayer, we feel the weight of being obsolete. In those times, it's important we remind ourselves of our value to the small circle of people in our lives. Sadly, in many church structures today that tend toward novelty and youth, older saints are suffering from relegation. What matters is the splash, the big ministry, the numbers—except this: thinking that way is anti-kingdom. Pouring your life into the circle God has brought around you is not only biblical; it's legacy-producing.

Experiencing Being Overlooked

Overwhelm can arise when we feel that we are mattering little in our everyday work. But the truth is that we matter simply because we bear the image of our Creator. He formed us in our mother's womb. He endows us with purpose. He imbues us with glory. And in a properly framed kingdom mindset, he can take what we offer and make something beautiful out of it. We don't need the moniker of youth or the splash of success or the glory of numbers to fill us. We simply need the nod of our Savior, reminding us that we work for him, for his renown. Whenever I look at worldly outcomes, I get discouraged, and the overwhelm seeps in. But when I remember that God's kingdom is upside down and often unseen, life becomes less worrisome and far more purposeful.

Truths About Rooted You

- God's kingdom doesn't measure things the world's system does.
- Our obedience to God may be God's means of saving someone else.
- No matter where you find yourself, God is there.
- In difficult marriages, God notices and has compassion on you.
- In crazy, scary situations, God will equip you to obey and persevere.

Questions for Discussion

1. What did you initially believe about Zipporah before you picked up this book?
2. What lessons from Zipporah's life most resonate with you?
3. Have you ever experienced a time when your obedience helped rescue another person from peril? What happened?
4. When (if) you have relocated, how did God show his faithfulness to you?
5. What cultural changes have taken place since Zipporah's time? What has remained the same?

CHAPTER THREE

Manoah's Wife, the Grieved One

Manoah's wife felt the pangs of living under the grip of Philistine might. No matter what she did, their circumstances confronted her with this ugly, daily reality, and she begged God for deliverance. As she gleaned the fields outside her town of Zorah, she recounted how the nation of Israel found itself in this dark predicament. She placed an errant sheave in her carrying basket, remembering how Israel had defied the Living God by chasing after idols, even when they were specifically warned again and again not to do so. It had become a cycle of pain, she knew. Rebellion. Consequences for that rebellion. Repentance, then redemption. As the sun broke down upon her, heating her brow and causing sweat and discomfort, she filled her basket and trudged homeward.

As she walked the dusty trail, she prayed. "Lord, please forgive us. Please rescue us from the might of the Philistines. We as a country need your redemption, and we need it soon, but it's our clan of Dan that seems to need it even more." As she neared her home, the familiar ache took over. Manoah was there, looking from the doorway with kind eyes and a bit of a stooped gait. Together they bore the pain of living under Philistine rule, but they also bore something much heavier: barrenness. She whispered a quick prayer, asking God to please unlock her womb before entering their home and making a meager meal of grain.

That night, the supper she ate burned her throat as it erupted from her stomach to her mouth. She swallowed, then went outside under a star-decorated sky. Not knowing what to do with her discomfort, she walked the familiar trail to the wide-open grain field she had gleaned in the day before. The moon winked at her from its place high in the sky. She ventured into the stalks of emmer wheat, now shorn by rabid Philistines, with very few kernels decorating the earth beneath her feet. She was alone.

And then she was not.

She turned to see a glowing being, twice her height, with a sword in its hand and fire emanating from large eyes. She jumped backward, terrified, then lost her footing and tripped, falling onto the field. She stood, righting herself. She meant to say something, but her tongue stuck to the roof of her mouth.

"Even though you have been unable to have children," the being said. "You will soon become pregnant and give birth to a son."

A son? Her? She shook her head, disbelieving such words.

But the being continued. "So be careful; you must not drink wine or any other alcoholic drink nor eat any forbidden food."

She nodded. Was this vision really happening? She shook her head, then steadied herself.

"You will become pregnant and give birth to a son," he repeated. "And his hair must never be cut. For he will be dedicated to God as a Nazirite from birth."

She knew the vow of the Nazirite and believed she could carry out such a task, particularly if it meant she would bear Manoah a child.

The being's eyes pierced her, ate through her, with a mixture of empathy and fortitude. "He will begin to rescue Israel from the Philistines," he said.

And then he was no more. The stars blinked above her as usual. The moon, though lower and smaller in the sky, still existed. She came to herself there, then ran to Manoah, shaking him awake in their tiny home.

He rubbed his eyes.

"A man of God appeared to me!" She could hear the histrionic rise in her voice, so she told herself to pace her words. "He looked like one of God's angels, terrifying to see."

"What?" Manoah asked. He shook his head as if trying to shake the sleep from his eyes.

"I didn't ask where he was from, and he didn't tell me his name. But he told me, 'You will become pregnant and give birth to a son. You must not drink wine or any other alcoholic drink nor eat any forbidden food. For your son will be dedicated to God as a Nazirite from the moment of his birth until the day of his death.'"

Manoah knelt by their bedside, then motioned for her to join him. He covered himself with his prayer shawl, then said, "Lord, please let the man of God come back to us again and give us more instructions about this son who is to be born."

46 The Most Overwhelmed Women of the Bible

The next day, she went to glean in the fields under a cloudy canopy. Thoughts of possible pregnancy, then the potential of delivering their deliverer, made her smile. As she picked up errant stalks, what she now knew as an angel suddenly appeared to her. He said nothing.

She remembered Manoah's earnest prayer and ran back to the village to alert him. He followed her back to the field where the angel stood—tall, glowing, and looming.

"Are you the man who spoke to my wife the other day?" he asked.

The angel nodded. "Yes," he replied, "I am."

"When your words come true, what kind of rules should govern the boy's life and work?"

Manoah's wife shook her head. She had already told Manoah everything this angel had told her.

The angel boomed, "Be sure your wife follows the instructions I gave her. She must not eat grapes or raisins, drink wine or any other alcoholic drink, or eat any forbidden food."

"Please stay here," Manoah said, "until we can prepare a young goat for you to eat."

"I will stay," the being said, "but I will not eat anything. However, you may prepare a burnt offering as a sacrifice to the Lord."

Later, Manoah's wife would realize that this was no normal encounter, nor was it merely an angelic visitation. They were not talking with a mortal, but God himself, disguised.

Still, Manoah persisted in his curiosity. "What is your name? For when all this comes true, we want to honor you."

"Why do you ask my name? It is too wonderful for you to understand."

While Manoah's wife pondered those words, Manoah quickly ran back to their home, corralled their goat, slaughtered it, drained it of its blood as was the custom, then brought the carcass to the field. He offered it upon a large stone at the field's edge.

Flames engulfed the goat's body as the wood crackled and spat. As the meat was consumed, the fire grew heavenward. At that precise moment, the being stepped into the ascending flames and disappeared into the sky.

In a moment, she found herself prostrate on the dusty earth, embers singeing her skin. Manoah lay next to her, stock still.

Eventually they sat up. A circle of ashes smoldered around the rock that had become a makeshift altar. Manoah lifted her to her feet. "We will certainly die," he said, his voice haggard. "For we have seen God!"

But she felt differently. After embracing Manoah, she pulled back. "If the Lord were going to kill us, he wouldn't have accepted our burnt offering and grain offering. He wouldn't have appeared to us and told us this wonderful thing and done these miracles."

Still, Manoah seemed to live in fear until the day she told him she was pregnant. He let out a breath then and relocated them to a new place, Mahaneh-dan, between Zorah and Eshtaol.

A few months later, she felt the clinching of her torso come in rhythmic contractions. It would be soon time to welcome their son into the world. When he muscled his way into the world, she named him Samson, "sun child." As she stroked his brow, she wondered what he would endure to free her people from the stranglehold of the Philistines.

<hr />

Samson grew as strong as his hair was long. But much to their distaste, he wanted to marry a Philistine woman whom he found attractive. Though she protested along with Manoah, Samson

48   The Most Overwhelmed Women of the Bible

would not be deterred, so they arranged the marriage in grief. A sense of foreboding invaded her mind. And yet? The marriage did not consummate because his wife-to-be betrayed his confidence by revealing a riddle to his attendants. Instead, his bride-to-be married his best man, unbeknownst to Samson.

So when Samson wanted to offer a young goat to the woman whom he thought would still be his wife, the girl's Philistine father told him they gave her to his best man. "I truly thought you must hate her," the Philistine said. "So I gave her in marriage to your best man. But look, her younger sister is even more beautiful than she is. Marry her instead."

He did not like such a deceptive offer, and it pained her to watch her son wrestle with the aftermath. Samson's anger fueled a strange attack instead. He destroyed the Philistine's olive groves and vineyards by tying foxes' tails together, binding each pair with a torch, and leveling the foliage with fire. And then he attacked the Philistines so viciously that his own countrymen retrieved Samson from the cave in the rock of Etam and delivered him to the Philistines. Manoah's wife worried for her son's fate, but then she remembered the word of the Lord—that he would deliver Judah from the might of the Philistines. It was only later that she heard he killed one thousand Philistines with the jaw of a donkey, and then he began his life as a judge for the nation.

Her son Samson did not obey the Lord God in the way he pursued women, though he had not been raised to stray this way, she knew. He visited a prostitute, then fell headlong in love with Delilah from the Sorek Valley—a woman who would prove to be her son's demise. Delilah revealed the secret of Samson's strength—his uncut hair—and the Philistines, in a rage, cut his strength, then gouged out Samson's eyes and imprisoned him with bronze chains in Gaza. When she heard of it, Manoah's wife wept. Samson, who was to be the deliverer of their countrymen, now spent his prison days grinding grain under cruel duress.

Still, she prayed. She reminded herself of the visit with the God who made all things, who saw all things, who knew all things. She met this God yet did not die—she, a humble servant, a nobody. She obeyed the mandates of avoiding wine, juice, grapes, and raisins—all for the sake of a son who was now bound. As long as Samson lived under her roof, she did not allow a razor to touch his head. Every prayer she prayed, she knew Samson's hair was growing back, and he would once again be stronger than a lion. Still, she grieved his condition and spent sleepless nights imagining what Samson was going through.

The evil god Dagon would be celebrated soon, where the Philistines would whip themselves into a frenzied state, praising a false god, a detestable idol. They offered pagan sacrifices, while Samson's mother watched. Officials proclaimed, "Our god has given us victory over our enemy Samson!"

But she knew their days were numbered.

Carousing and drunk, one crowd member roared, "Bring out Samson so he can amuse us!"

She cringed inwardly, watching from afar. And then she prayed God would be gracious with his promises.

"We will see him," she said to no one. Manoah had been buried amongst his fathers years prior, and she still had not grown accustomed to his absence and sometimes spoke to empty air. Her words were more pleading than prayer, a longing for things to be right not only for the nation, but for her son, whose sight had been gouged.

Officials manhandled Samson, but she could see a brief smile play upon his lips. Samson's strength had indeed returned. They positioned him between the pillars holding up Dagon's temple roof.

Seeing him without his beautiful eyes, though, wrenched her heart, igniting fresh grief. Samson had to ask a young servant boy to lead him.

She moved closer as Samson told the servant, "Place my hands against the pillars that hold up the temple. I want to rest against them."

She took in the sight, her heart heavy. Where Samson was positioned, if he tested his strength, the building would crush him. Thousands of people stood on the roof above him, and thousands taunted him in the temple's courtyard. Jeers erupted from above and below, asking Samson to amuse them with his so-called feats, then mocking him when he did nothing.

She swallowed. Held her breath. Held her grief in check.

Samson looked toward the heavens then, though where eyes should have been, gouges lived. He opened his mouth and prayed, "Sovereign Lord, remember me again. O God, please strengthen me just one more time."

"Yes, Lord," she said quietly.

Samson cleared his throat. "With one blow let me pay back the Philistines for the loss of my two eyes."

With those words, she forced herself to flee. As best she could, she picked through the crowd away from the giant building. She turned to see Samson's hands pushing the two great pillars. They began to buckle. "Let me die with the Philistines," he shouted.

"No." She did not want such a fate for her beloved son. Though she had other sons after him—each one a miracle and blessing from the Most High God—Samson had captured her heart as her first-born after a long, lonely barrenness. But as the building quaked beneath the ripple of his muscles, she knew this to be the strange fulfillment of God's declaration over her son. He would be a deliverer, but in a difficult twist of events, his deliverance would mean the sacrifice of his life.

In one hellish crash, the building buckled, then toppled onto Samson and all the Philistines and their leaders. Later, she learned Samson had killed more Philistines in his death than he ever had in his life.

Her sons worked day and night to recover Samson's body in the rubble of the temple. They buried him between Zorah and Eshtaol in Manoah's tomb, while she cried tears of gratitude and loss for a terribly beautiful promise fulfilled.

The Biblical Narrative

The story of Manoah's wife and her son Samson can be found in Judges 13–16.

Did you know the Philistines (and who they were) gave us the word *Palestine*? And—as you are probably even more aware—there is still conflict between Israelites and Palestinians. This people group who oppressed the Israelites for forty years during the time of the judges were pagan idol worshipers, paying homage to Dagon (which you saw in the above narrative), Baal-zebub, and Ashtaroth. They were uncircumcised, and they conquered others because of their ability to wield metal (metallurgy). When you read the Old Testament, particularly when God warns the nation of Israel of what *not* to worship, these gods are often listed. Sadly, the Israelites practiced syncretism, which is a folding in of other religions and worship practices alongside the worship of Yahweh. Like eating a chocolate brownie laced with excrement, worshiping little gods alongside *the* God of the universe contaminates the whole treat.

Interestingly, the Jewish people were somewhat satisfied with their captors because they didn't want Samson to mess with their "peace." They were the ones to deliver Samson back into the hands of their captors. This reveals just how at ease they became with this foreign, idol-loving, warfaring nation.

In the middle of all this conquest and odd conciliation, we see Manoah's wife interrupt the scene. She is barren (*'aqar*) which simply means she could not get pregnant. She joins a pantheon of other women in the Old Testament who also battled this condition: Sarah, Rebekah, Rachel, and, later, Hannah. All their children played important roles in saving the nation (Isaac, Jacob, Joseph, and the prophet Samuel.) Isn't it interesting that an impossible situation begets unusual deliverance—where only God can get the glory?

But there is another interesting parallel if we jump to the New Testament to the birth of John the Baptist. Consider their similarities: Barren women were visited by a supernatural being (a theophany, or "God appearance" in Manoah's wife's case, and the angel Gabriel in Elizabeth's). Both were promised a son who would adhere to a Nazirite code. Both sons were empowered mightily—Samson with supernatural strength, and John the Baptist with fiery preaching and prophetic words. Both were martyred. Samson preceded the era of the kings. John the Baptist preceded the era of the King of kings.

Back to the text. The Hebrew word for behold is *hinneh*. It's that part of speech in English known as an interjection like "Wow" or "Yikes." This is the first word spoken to Manoah's wife when God interrupts her life. Charles Spurgeon elaborates, "'Behold' is a word of wonder; it is intended to excite admiration. Wherever you see it hung out in Scripture, it is like an ancient signboard,

Manoah's Wife, the Grieved One 53

signifying that there are rich wares within, or like the hands which solid readers have observed in the margin of the older Puritanic books, drawing attention to something particularly worthy of observation."[1] After this *behold*, everything changes for Manoah's wife. Not only will her barrenness be reversed, but her offspring will bring deliverance.

But there is a caveat. He will be a Nazirite. For a more in-depth study of what this means, read Numbers 6. There we learn that those who want to take a specific vow of a Nazirite must refrain from any product of the grapevine, including grapes and vinegar, and they must not cut their hair or touch a dead body. These terms, however, were short—the vow was made for a specific period of time. But in this case with Manoah's wife and her son Samson, his would be a vow for life. And since she would be carrying this deliverer, she also had to refrain from grape-related products as well.

Her encounter with the angelic being could certainly be a theophany—a visitation of the preincarnate Christ. And it's quite interesting that he appeared to Manoah's wife outside of Manoah's presence. Twice she is visited, and had she not retrieved Manoah the second time, he would not have experienced this divine encounter. It's also interesting that this theophany affirmed Manoah's wife's first encounter in saying, "Be sure your wife follows the instructions I gave her" (Judges 13:13a). And when Manoah boldly asks the angel's name, he responds this way: "'Why do you ask my name?' the angel of the Lord replied. 'It is too wonderful for you to understand'" (Judges 13:18). The word here for *wonderful* is instructive, *peliy*. This specific word is only used one other time in the Old Testament, in Psalm 139:6. "Such knowledge is too *wonderful* for me, too great for me to understand" (emphasis mine). Another form of it is used in the well-known passage Isaiah 9:6b: "And he will be called: Wonderful Counselor . . ." All of this underscores the profound otherness of this divine encounter. It is far beyond their contemplation, above their understanding. Imagine the overwhelm that would happen in a God-touching-earth moment like this! Later, in Judges 13:19, a form of this word is used, *pala*, which is translated as *wonders*. In the NLT, it's translated as *amazing*. "The Lord did an amazing thing." The God of wonders does wonderful things. Our amazing God can't help but perform amazing deeds.

And this encounter they both had demonstrates the outlandish power of God. He ascends flames (impossible) and returns to the heavens. This encounter was so awe-inspiring that they fell face down to the ground. It's also interesting to note that while Manoah recognized they had seen God and would therefore die, Manoah's wife reasoned that away when she reminded him that in that awesome display, God did accept their offering, and he had a purpose for them because he appeared to them. They did end up surviving, and God's promise to Manoah's wife (twice!) came true with the birth of Samson. The person who named him wasn't his father, but his mother who gave him a moniker that meant "sun, sunlight, or brightness." It's a fascinating name, particularly knowing that two miles across the plains of Sorek was a village called Beth-Shemesh, where the inhabitants worshiped the sun god.[2]

What Does This Mean for Overwhelmed You?

What You Were Once Does Not Mean You Will Forever Be That Way

God is the God of the great reversal. You may have lived overwhelmed (for a variety of reasons), but God's heart is to fulfill Psalm 23 in your life—to lead you to a quiet, peaceful place and grant you rest. The NET translation of Judges 13:3 is instructive here, where

God reverses Manoah's wife's fortunes. "You are infertile and child-less, but you will conceive and have a son." She was two things prior, but the reversal would happen after God's intervention—non-barren and son-holding.

In the New Testament, we see a similar reversal in 1 Corinthians 6:11: "Some of you were once like that. But you were cleansed; you were made holy; you were made right with God by calling on the name of the Lord Jesus Christ and by the Spirit of our God." The verses prior outline what people were like before meeting Christ—enslaved to sin. That word "but" is the fulcrum upon which the change happens. You were once one way, and now because of Jesus and his intervention in your life, you are now another way. Peter emphasizes this reversal of fortune when he writes, "Once you had no identity as a people; now you are God's people. Once you received no mercy; now you have received God's mercy" (1 Peter 2:10). All that to say who you were is not who you will be. Not because of your ability to overcome your overwhelmed feelings, but because God can do the miraculous in your midst. From broken to whole. From overwhelmed to comforted.

The Overwhelm of Another's Choices

When we think of the life of the wife of Manoah, we can't help but wonder how it must've been for her to watch Samson make some awful choices. He didn't want a wife from their own tribe (Dan) but demanded a Philistine wife who ended up not becoming his wife because of her father's betrayal. This ushered in bloodshed upon the Philistines, which would have meant he violated the Nazirite vow of not touching the dead. He also touched the carcass of a lion, another forbidden act for an Israelite—and a Nazirite. He solicited a prostitute. He pursued another Philistine woman, Delilah. He disclosed his Nazirite secret (about his hair being his source of strength), which then led to his terrible demise—eye-gouging and imprisonment. Mothers bear the pain of their children's choices, and those decisions can quickly overwhelm any mother. Have you ever felt that way? Have you walked the grief trail of your adult children's choices like Manoah's wife?

I wrote a book about this kind of overwhelm entitled *Love, Pray, Listen: Parenting Your Wayward Adult Kids with Joy.* Mothers who experience the rebellion of their children have their own kind of angst and pain. And yet, I get the feeling from the Scriptures that Manoah's wife remained steadfast during all of Samson's wanderings. No child is perfect. No human can make great decisions every day of their lives. She had experienced the very voice of God telling her (promising her!) that her son would be a deliverer—that he would rescue the Israelites from the Philistinian oppression. I can only imagine the slow realization she must've come to when she took note of Samson's strengthening arms holding up a temple that, if it fell, would destroy many Philistines. She not only experienced deliverance then, but that deliverance meant sacrifice for her son.

When we come to the end of ourselves and we cannot make our children choose the path we prefer, we still can reach out to the One whose *every* child rebelled. God the Father, the perfect parent, provided a perfect environment for his first two children, yet they rebelled. And they continued that spree of rebellion up until this very moment. Billions upon billions of his children (all of them) have rebelled. Because God loves us so much, he grants us the gift of free will, which we all really appreciate, but not so much when our children start exercising it. All that to say, God deeply understands the overwhelm of straying children. He has empathy for parents in that space.

So many psalms display a reaching toward God in times of deep sadness, overwhelm, and distress. Consider Psalm 61:1–4: "O God, listen to my cry! Hear my prayer! From the ends of the earth, I cry to you for help when my heart is overwhelmed. Lead me to the towering rock of safety, for you are my safe refuge, a fortress where my enemies cannot reach me. Let me live forever in your sanctuary, safe beneath the shelter of your wings!" When you're experiencing the overwhelm that comes from other people's destructive choices, there is a Rock you can run to, a shelter in the storm of your spiraling thoughts.

Death Is the Final Overwhelm

Manoah's wife also felt the overwhelm of the death of a loved one. Grief is its own kind of overwhelming feeling—it pervades our lives, steals our joy, and infuses our lack of motivation. It's not enough to stuff it down and pretend all is well. We must deal with it head on. Like the psalmist does above, we can reach toward the Lord when we grieve. But we must also reach horizontally. It's instructive that Manoah's wife had community around her at his death. "Later his brothers and other relatives went down to get his body. They took him back home and buried him between Zorah and Eshtaol, where his father, Manoah, was buried" (Judges 16:31). We, too, need community when we're grieving. I'm currently walking through a season of grief, but I too often find myself isolating in that grief. The more I push community away, the lonelier and more broken I feel. While it's normal to cocoon after a loss, it's not beneficial in the long run because you have no one to help shoulder your grief or listen to your pain.

Our Callings Can Be Overwhelming

The calling on Manoah's wife, which initially involved abstaining from all grape products, most likely remained upon her, particularly as she watched her son fulfill his own calling, albeit hesitantly (or

58   The Most Overwhelmed Women of the Bible

recklessly) at times. Having a calling on our lives can be its own concoction of overwhelm. We may feel like we're not measuring up. We may obsess over our inability to fulfill it. We may mourn lost potential as we age. We may look at other people's callings and envy those, forgetting that God uniquely gifts and calls each of us on our own specific, unique journeys. We may find our callings small, or maybe even burdensome. Thankfully, we can rest in knowing that it is God's faithfulness, not our perfection, that enables us to step into our callings.

Paul not only encourages us in our callings, but he also defines them in his first letter to the Thessalonians. He begins with didactic instruction in verses 14–22 of chapter 5. These commands are connected to our calling in the same way obedience is connected to our fruitfulness:

- Warn those who are lazy.
- Encourage those who are timid.
- Take tender care of those who are weak.
- Be patient with everyone.
- See that no one pays back evil for evil.
- Always try to do good to each other and all people.
- Always be joyful.
- Never stop praying.
- Be thankful in all circumstances.
- Do not stifle the Holy Spirit.
- Do not scoff at prophecies.
- Test everything that is said.
- Hold on to what is good.
- Stay away from every kind of evil.

Of course, none of these actions can be accomplished in our own strength, and perhaps that's the point. Manoah's wife had an encounter with the living God, and that connection, no doubt, helped her endure a difficult calling. Watch how Paul commissions the Thessalonians after this powerful list of obedience: "Now may the God of peace make you holy in every way, and may your whole spirit and soul and body be kept blameless until our Lord Jesus Christ comes again. God will make this happen, for he who calls you is faithful" (1 Thessalonians 5:23–24). God was faithful to his words to Manoah's wife. She fulfilled her calling, and he orchestrated events so that Samson would fulfill his. Samson, though often faithless, could not thwart God's redemptive plan.

When you're discouraged that you may have messed everything up in a lapse of disobedience, remember this: You're not that powerful. God can use even your failures to accomplish his redemptive plan. Your only position is that of humbleness—to surrender afresh to him, seek his voice, and honor him as he enables you to do the next right thing.

Truths About Comforted You

- In your desperation, God takes note of your prayers and pleas.
- Your joy is not dependent on the obedience of another.
- Grief is a long, painful journey, and it's best to process it both vertically (with the Lord) and horizontally (with others).
- You cannot thwart the plan of God.
- God's character can be counted on, even when others demonstrate a lack of character.

Questions for Discussion

1. What surprised you about this story? Had you remembered it, in terms of Manoah's wife?
2. Have you ever had a supernatural experience of God, or have you known someone who has? What happened?
3. Why do you think Manoah's wife also had to carry out the Nazirite vow?
4. In what ways does this story reveal the character of God?
5. What new historical fact did you learn during this chapter? What did you learn about the time of the judges?

CHAPTER FOUR

Naaman's Slave Girl, the Imprisoned One

During the time of Elisha the prophet, when Hazael reigned over Aram-Damascus, his forces abducted her, a young Israeli girl, giving her to his commander's wife as a help-maid. She had no volition in this new state of subjugation, but she did know her God. And this proved to be her strength, she knew.

The day of her abduction commenced like any sunshiny morning—the birds whistled their songs in the orchard, her father's melody lilting throughout their homestead. She had tended their sheep and goats, milked the nannies, and returned the milk to Mother, who would turn it into cheese and whey. Their lives centered on God and land—living in the promises of Yahweh, who delivered her people from the hand of the Egyptians. Through unstable times, she felt joy in her little enclave of *shalom*.

She felt the rousing of hoofbeats through her feet that stayed anchored to the earthen floor of her home as she kneaded bread for her family. With brothers to feed, the work of satisfying them took everyone's efforts. She left the front door of their modest home, then strained her eyes toward the eastern horizon as the sun ventured toward the center of the sky. Dust obscured whoever it was who came their way—almost appearing like a swarm of gnats.

"Calm yourself," Mother said, coming up alongside her. "All will be well. Just remain peaceful."

She thought it an odd thing to say in the moment. After all, no one knew what this clop of hooves and cloud of dust meant. At least that's what she thought as she looked into Mother's frightened eyes. "What is wrong?"

"Raiders," Mother said. "Hide yourself. I need to warn your brothers." With that, her mother ran from the house while she hid herself beneath her parents' bed, heart pounding.

It was the shouting in a foreign tongue—a language that sounded more like spitting than speaking—that stopped her heart. She peeked from beneath the bed to see boots trampling upon their home and chairs overturning amid shouting and laughter.

She pleaded with God then, asking him to hide her forever under the coverlets. But God did not oblige her prayer. In that moment, a man with ire in his eyes upended the bed, exposing her. With one smooth motion, he pulled her to her feet, barked something that she could only interpret as "move," and shoved her out into the bird-song air. Except the birds had flown clear away; they were clever like that. She looked everywhere, scanning the hills of her land, but she could not see Father or Mother or her brothers. "Keep them safe," she prayed in Hebrew.

The hooves that had stirred up dirt now provided the mount beneath her. For days they traveled on, away from home, far from normalcy under the heat of an unrelenting sun. She constantly

Naaman's Slave Girl, the Imprisoned One 63

looked behind her, hoping to see Father racing to rescue her, but eventually she faced forward toward a fate she could not anticipate.

When they arrived at a compound days later, one of the men pulled her violently from her saddle, then shoved her forward into the arms of a woman who tsked, then shook her head. The woman brought her into her home, showed her a small room, then motioned for her to cook and clean. Eventually she understood enough of the language to know she was in Syria in the home of a well-known soldier—a commander, actually. He was away for the first few months of her enslavement, but when he returned, she was surprised to find Naaman a leper. Every part of her knew the laws of her Lord, that those with leprosy were unclean in her culture and would have to live outside the camp, but here stood a leprous warrior, living with his family. Though she prayed often for rescue, she grew to empathize with the constant pain he experienced and the necessary care he endured because of his condition.

She had often learned this truth about the world: people who did great feats had great weaknesses, and in Naaman's case, it was leprosy.

Helpless to escape her lot, she prayed and asked the Lord of Israel for insight and help. Perhaps, she thought, Naaman's leprosy fueled his conquests. What did he have to lose? Still, God fell silent as she prayed. Until one day.

When she remembered.

While Elijah the prophet performed miracles and proclaimed the greatness of their God, it had been rumored that Elisha had asked God for a double share of his spirit—and God had granted it. He had divided a river, cleansed impure water, commanded lions, assisted in seemingly impossible battles, provided miraculously for an impoverished widow, opened the womb of a barren lady, then resurrected her son from death. He represented the power of God, and it seemed whatever he touched became a miracle.

The Lord saw fit to remind her of all these feats at once. As she prepared the midday meal, she spoke to her mistress. "I wish my master would go to see the prophet in Samaria. He would heal him of his leprosy." Her mistress's eyes widened, then she rushed from the room. In a moment, Naaman entered, regaled in armor, but with decaying fingers.

He asked about this magician and what sort of powers he had.

"He has brought a boy from death to life," she said. But she did not name the prophet.

That evening Naaman returned from his visit with King Hazael. He spoke to his wife, while the servant girl listened. "He has given me permission to visit the prophet," he said.

"How will you know who it is, and why would our enemy help us?" his wife asked.

"The king wrote this."

From around the corner, she noticed a scroll.

"The king wrote a letter of introduction—to bring to the king of Israel." He unrolled it, then read, "With this letter I present my servant Naaman. I want you to heal him of his leprosy." He rolled it back up, then pointed to a pile of objects covered with a shawl. "He's given me 750 pounds of silver, 150 pounds of gold, and ten sets of clothing as gifts."

"May the gods be with us, dear Naaman," his wife said. Then she helped him pack the king's gifts and motioned for her to accompany the group on their trek to Samaria—"After all," she said to her servant girl, "You know the area and the culture."

Naaman directly approached Israel's king, something she would not have done, but she had little voice in the matter. She did hear the king's desperation, however.

Naaman's Slave Girl, the Imprisoned One 65

Surrounded by gifts, he wiped his brow, then looked heavenward. "Am I God, that I can give life and take it away? Why is this man asking me to heal someone with leprosy? I can see he's just trying to pick a fight with me."

But thankfully, Elisha, who seemed to always know all things, had sent a message to the king while Naaman was still there, leprous and curious.

The king read the scroll: "Why are you so upset? Send Naaman to me, and he will learn there is a true prophet here in Israel."

Their entourage, which consisted of chariots, horses, and gifts, soon made their way to the door of Elisha. Naaman lifted his leprous hand and knocked. Instead of Elisha, a messenger greeted him. "My master says this: Go and wash yourself seven times in the Jordan River. Then your skin will be restored, and you will be healed of your leprosy."

The servant girl let out her breath. All would be well. Whatever Elisha said would come to pass.

Unfortunately, Naaman was too proud to submit himself to such illogical instructions. He motioned for his wife. "I thought he would certainly come out to meet me!"

She tried to reason with him, but he shushed her.

"I expected him to wave his hand over the leprosy and call on the name of the Lord his God and heal me! Aren't the rivers of Damascus, the Abana and the Pharpar, better than the rivers of Israel? Why shouldn't I wash in them and be healed?" He roused his horse and turned away in a huff.

So she prayed. She knew Elisha's words would make a difference in Naaman's life, if only he would submit to them. Thankfully, his officers pulled him aside before he could race back to Syria. "Sir," one said—quite bravely, she thought, "if the prophet had told you to do something very difficult, wouldn't you have done it? So you should certainly obey him when he says simply 'Go and wash and be cured!'"

66   The Most Overwhelmed Women of the Bible

Naaman let out a long breath, then directed his horse back toward the Jordan. He removed his outer garments, then dunked into the healing waters seven times. Before their eyes, his white skin pinked, and he was fully, powerfully restored.

What joy it was to be a part of one man's restoration, she thought. But more than that, she felt the smile of God upon her.

Cleansed, he returned to Elisha.

This time the prophet came to the door.

Naaman bowed before him. "Now I know that there is no God in all the world except in Israel." He pointed to the chariot full of fine metals and clothing. "These are for you."

"As surely as the Lord lives, whom I serve, I will not accept any gifts."

"I insist," he said.

But Elisha held his ground.

Naaman pointed to the ground. "All right, but please allow me to load two of my mules with earth from this place, and I will take it back home with me. From now on I will never again offer burnt offerings or sacrifices to any other god except the Lord."

The servant girl rejoiced. Though she could not secure her freedom, she would now be working with a man who feared the Lord.

Naaman kicked at the earth. "May the Lord pardon me this one thing: When my master the king goes into the temple of the god Rimmon to worship there and leans on my arm, may the Lord pardon me when I bow, too."

The prophet pronounced peace on Naaman.

And she felt it in her bones.

The Biblical Narrative

You will find the story of Naaman's slave girl (unnamed), a Samaritan, in 2 Kings 5. Although it is not mentioned whether she

Naaman's Slave Girl, the Imprisoned One   67

accompanied his entourage to see Elisha, I took authorial license to make it so. Whether she witnessed his healing is not as important as knowing she would have eventually learned the story of it after he was healed.

The truth is that she knew God's abilities. She knew his power wielded through his prophets. And although she was enslaved, she still sought the good of the one she was enslaved to.

A close reading of the passage shows some misunderstanding. Although she was clear that Naaman needed to see the prophet, he instead, armed with a letter from the Syrian king, approaches Israel's king instead. He asks the impossible—that the king would heal him. Thankfully, the prophet Elisha, the mentee of Elijah, sends him a message of healing. As you read above, Naaman initially poo-poos this nonsense, preferring the waters of his home country to the smallness and insignificance of the Jordan river and the pedestrian, non-spectacular request that he simply wash himself.

Cooler heads prevail in the form of his servants and advisors; he washes and is then cleansed.

He would not have started this journey had it not been for the words of the unnamed slave girl. She is from Samaria, the northern kingdom of Israel during the time of the prophets—a period also detailed in 2 Chronicles 10–20. Broadly, this is the time between the kingdom of Solomon until the time of the Babylonian captivity—an era of rampant idol worship, warnings from many prophets, and apostasy.

And in the middle of what could be a historical footnote, this girl emulates Joseph in Egypt or Esther in Persia—as an unlikely missionary to a pagan people. In many ways, she embodied what a later prophet would encourage Israelites to do in Babylon: "And work for the peace and prosperity of the city where I sent you into exile. Pray to the Lord for it, for its welfare will determine your welfare" (Jeremiah 29:7). She reflects the heart of God, who had

68 The Most Overwhelmed Women of the Bible

always reached beyond the nation to the whole world. In a very real sense, she is a missionary, albeit a captive one.

This servant girl hints at what is to come—a time when Jesus will walk the earth, heal the outcasts, and cure leprosy. She reveals God's sovereign ways, plans we don't always recognize or perceive. Her owner, Naaman, is again mentioned in Luke chapter 4 with this idea of sovereignty:

> Certainly there were many needy widows in Israel in Elijah's time, when the heavens were closed for three and a half years, and a severe famine devastated the land. Yet Elijah was not sent to any of them. He was sent instead to a foreigner—a widow of Zarephath in the land of Sidon. And many in Israel had leprosy in the time of the prophet Elisha, but the only one healed was Naaman, a Syrian. When they heard this, the people in the synagogue were furious. (Luke 4:25–28)

Their furor revealed that they felt Israel was God's only delight, that he would save them solely from the iron fist of the Roman empire. When Jesus mentions these two prophets and who they helped, the Jewish leaders grew angry. God should not care about Sidonians or Syrians. That Jesus mentioned this messed with their categories of who God would bless.

What Does This Mean for Overwhelmed You?

Slavery Means Overwhelm
Although many of us have not experienced slavery, it continues to be a horrific problem, with some estimates that nearly 50 million

people worldwide are slaves, 25 percent of which are children.[1] Antislavery.org defines modern slavery "as when an individual is exploited by others, for personal or commercial gain. Whether tricked, coerced, or forced, they lose their freedom. This includes but is not limited to human trafficking, forced labour [sic] and debt bondage."[2] Certainly, in this unnamed girl's instance, she was kidnapped and forced to work for another, living without freedom in a foreign land.

Overwhelm would not begin to describe what she must have been feeling. She was forced to live outside her country, away from her parents, now living with people who spoke an entirely different language who were idolators and conquerors. Her captors were enemies of her nation, and they no doubt had ill intent toward her—and if not ill intent, then outright neglect. She had no advocate, no voice, no volition.

Those entrapped in abusive marriages face a similar overwhelm. Or those who have experienced past sexual abuse. Or those whose economics force them to live in unsafe places. These are people who are suffering *not* because of their choices, but because of the malicious intent of others bent on oppressing them, or simply being in the wrong place at the wrong time. In the case of the slave girl, she had no way of freeing herself but had to live within the parameters of her confinement. Many who are currently abused may have the opportunity to leave but may still feel unable to free themselves from an abusive situation.

Keeping the Faith

In that state of constant overwhelm, how can we learn from Naaman's slave girl? First, she did not delete her faith. Though enslaved in an idolatrous land, she remembered who she was—that she was one of God's chosen people, and that God loved to act on behalf of his people. No doubt she had heard the narratives of God freeing her people from Egyptian slavery. The narrative had been shared and passed down through oral tradition and the celebration of the Passover. She contemplated the truth that God would still do the miraculous through his prophets.

We live in an era of untangling of beliefs, where people are revisiting their relationships with church and God. The world pushes against belief, and it entices us to stray. Like the servant girl, we have a choice to remember God's faithfulness—to look back and remind ourselves of God's power, particularly when we are surrounded by confusion and a culture of disbelief. One of the greatest critiques of the nation of Israel was its seeming inability to remember, to ponder the greatness of God in the past. Whenever I'm tempted to throw in the towel, I try to look back and remember all the amazing things God has already done in my life. That story of faithfulness helps me navigate my current stress.

God's Reach Is Global

The servant girl also had a high view of God's compassion that extended to the whole world, not merely her nation. She viewed the plight of her captors and offered them a very real solution. Had she not talked about the prophet who could bring healing, Naaman wouldn't have started the journey toward his own miracle (which, in a way, preserved her; she would no longer be exposed to leprosy). She understood God's call to Abraham—that the nation would be blessed in order to be a blessing to the entire cosmos.

Impossible Situations

Where she differs from some modern people is that there was most likely no way she could escape her lot. Some today do choose to free themselves from an abusive marriage, for example, which is its own exodus moment, though not simple or easy. Hers was an impossible situation. I remember this quote I penned in my journal in college when I dreamed of being a missionary: "When God wants to do an impossible task, he chooses an impossible person and breaks her." Certainly, this slave girl was facing an impossible situation, and her prospects were nil. God used her vulnerability to speak up to do the impossible.

How she moved from enslaved girl to rescuer is astonishing. Somehow, she pushed beyond her own predicament toward embracing empathy for the people who enslaved her. Only God could empower such a feat. Hers is a lesson in healing from trauma—it must be done, but it takes time. You hope that someday all that fear and pain will make you more empathetic toward the needs of others. In a very real sense, Naaman was enslaved to his condition, so she took her own state as a jumping-off point to serve him.

When you're enslaved but loved by God, deep down you are free. And you long to see others experience the beauty of the One who freed you. That journey takes time. It is not linear nor easy. But it is a necessary pathway.

We are not told how long it took between this girl's enslavement and her conversation about the prophet, but we can deduce that she most likely changed her perspective in that in-between time, moving from shock and pain to asking the question, "How can I be of benefit?"

Lest you think I'm promoting learning how to thrive in abusive situations, please hear me: If you are in an abusive situation, remember that God loves you and wants you to be whole and safe. Reach out however you can; call an abuse hotline; find good people who will help you find safety. In this case with the slave girl, unless she escaped (risky), she could not better her situation. In choosing to share about the prophet, this was possibly her way of making

72   The Most Overwhelmed Women of the Bible

the most of an untenable kidnapping. Her ability to think beyond herself was quite miraculous.

When You're Hurt by Others

There have been many times in my life when I have been overwhelmed by the choices of others. Through no volition of my own, I found myself trapped by someone else's sin. In one instance, it took me six years to work through that pain, and to be honest, I am still working through it. There were times I allowed the words and actions of another to derail me from the things God had for me to do. That person's actions brought on a lot of anxiety and feelings of depression. So when I look back on that traumatic interaction, I am quite amazed at this Israeli slave girl who seemingly rose above her dire circumstances to salve the wounds of another.

Moving from Trauma to Empathy

One of the most significant parts of my own journey of healing involves an outward focus. There were years that my childhood full of trauma retraumatized me in adulthood. This is quite normal, as trauma has a long tail. But there came a point where I longed (finally) to be set free from those bully triggers because they tethered me to a reality that no longer existed. I had to finally say, "This was the past. It is done. I cannot change it. I can only deal with what I face today." When I got to that point, my heart began to heal. God gently led me toward light, away from the dim realities of the past. And in that healing journey, the light dawned not merely on me, but also opened my eyes to the predicaments of others. When I started using that pain to empathize with people in my world, the trauma subsided. I began to see there was a "so-what" to all that mess.

The Scripture is silent on whether this kind of dynamic happened with the slave girl, but it is true that she looked outward,

Naaman's Slave Girl, the Imprisoned One 73

felt the pain of her captor, and sought to relieve that pain. She was emancipated internally to emancipate him externally. With her mindset shift, she was able to look beyond her own situation with benevolence as her motivation.

When I'm overwhelmed by my own past pain, I have found it helpful to grieve it, yes, but also to look for others who are also walking through hardship. I recently messaged a friend on the other side of the world who has walked through ministry hurt. I wanted to know how she was coping with it. Why? Because as I write this, I am walking through the valley of church hurt, and my eyes are better opened to that kind of pain in others. A lot of my writing has been around that space, and although it's been hard to see how many people have had the experience of church or ministry abuse or hurt, it is heartening that my own pain can fuel my empathy for others and bring relief.

Overwhelm hits us deeply when we are harmed by others mainly because we perceive that our agency has been taken away from us. I think of Jesus's question to the disciples when there were five thousand hungry men (plus women and children) to feed. In Mark 6:38, we read, "How many loaves do you have?" he asked. "Go and see." Jesus didn't ask them to give what they did not have, but what they did. And the result was a miraculous feeding. I'm not much for formulas, but in this case, the "formula" was their small piece plus God's great power equaled a large crowd fully satisfied. We see this same dynamic when Moses interacted with the Lord. "Then the LORD asked him, 'What is that in your hand?' 'A shepherd's staff,' Moses replied" (Exodus 4:2). God partnered with Moses through what little he held.

Perhaps you feel this way today while reading this chapter. You look in your hand and see only a few loaves or a couple fish or a walking stick. Those may seem small and inconsequential, but God uses your willingness to give him who you are in this moment to

74 The Most Overwhelmed Women of the Bible

do miraculous work through you. And when he does, he gets the glory. Look at how this story with the slave girl unfolded. A pagan warrior bent the knee to the one and only True God. Perhaps our mindset should change from what we can't do to what God can do through our overwhelm.

Truths About Emancipated You

- Sometimes we find ourselves in situations outside of our control because of the sinful actions of others.
- Growth comes when we ask God to move us from always looking backward to choosing to look forward.
- When we concentrate on what we don't have, we lose sight of what we do have in our hands.
- God's heart is for the whole world, not just a chosen few.
- God does miraculous work through our small obedience.

Questions for Discussion

1. Do you recall ever reading about this slave girl?
2. How does her bold proclamation (about God's ability to heal) encourage you today?
3. What past pain has held you back from helping others today?
4. What did you learn about the character of God from this story?
5. Naaman reveals pride when he (at first) refuses to wash in the Jordan river. In what ways have you battled pride this last month?

CHAPTER FIVE

Huldah, the Burdened One

Huldah took note of the transition in the New Quarter of Jerusalem, particularly as the Lord began speaking words over and through her. When Manasseh started his reign poorly, then repented, she watched the *hesed* of God pardon him, letting his life end well in light of his humility. Still, Jerusalem began to tumult when the king's son Amon took the throne. Her grandfather-in-law, Harhas, had been the keeper of the Temple wardrobe, and his stories of both royal and priestly corruption made their usual narrative pathways to his son Tikvah, then to her husband Shallum. They knew the tales of rising and falling, of goodness and corruption. And all through this hill-and-valley route Judah took, Huldah heard from God.

The conspiracy of his own officials against Amon? She knew.

His ultimate demise? God had let her in on that.

The coronation of eight-year-old Josiah? She knew that too.

But as Huldah attended to the needs of her family and kneaded dough for the day, she thought of the yeast of her nation, how a little bit of leaven, even the most miniscule amount, could raise the pulverized grains of wheat in the heat of day.

She spent her days like this—feeding, cleaning, attending to duties befitting a woman of valor—but whenever she could, she would drop to her knees or fall prostrate on the dusty floor of their home and seek the wisdom and word of the Almighty. For twelve years she interceded for young Josiah, and although he showed signs of following in the footsteps of the long dead King David, she worried for him. Today as her nose touched the earth, the word of the Lord came again, and it was strikingly like the word that had arrived in her ears (and heart). Judah would be punished for its blatant idolatry, its intermixing with the godless nations it had been told to conquer. This dread settled in on her like an over-wet woolen shawl in winter. It shivered her, permeated her bones, informed her mood.

A prophetess, if truly speaking the words of God, is not welcomed—not in her own country, in particular—when her words pronounce doom. She stood, punched down the risen dough, then exhaled as she walked into the outer court of their home. A fly buzzed around her, irritating her. She swatted at it, only to have the pest rally its family to torment her further. She covered her face with her hands. "Oh dear God, why have you chosen me to speak such words?"

At that precise moment, an entourage from the castle approached. She could see their insignias and the way they walked; these were royals. She swallowed, returned to her home, and shaped the loaf, hoping perhaps that these messengers had business with someone else. But the knock sounded, and she opened the door to five men, one of which she knew well—Hilkiah the priest.

Huldah, the Burdened One

"Huldah," he said. "This is Ahikam, Acbor, Shaphan, and Asaiah."

All bowed.

She returned the favor.

"Acbor is the son of Micaiah," Hilkiah said.

She nodded and welcomed them in. She swallowed. Though she knew in her gut what these officials wanted from her, she felt the familiar pang of fear. She tried to stifle it. As a prophetess, she knew well enough that she had to obey God, no matter what messages he conveyed through her. She directed the men to sit.

"Ahikam is the son of Shaphan," the priest said, pointing to him. "And Shaphan is the court secretary." He motioned toward the last man. "This is Asaiah, and he's King Josiah's personal advisor."

"So I have the privilege of welcoming some important men," she said. She offered them water from her water pot, but they all declined. "What do you want with me?" she asked.

Hilkiah explained that after Josiah ordered repairs to be carried out in the Temple, he had discovered the Book of the Law in the Temple's bowels. He handed the parchment to Shaphan who read it, then brought it to King Josiah.

"I read the scroll to the King," Shaphan said.

"And what happened?" Huldah asked. She remained standing as the men sat.

"He tore his clothes. He despaired. His demeanor was that of extreme alarm. So he told us to go to the Temple to speak to the Lord about this scroll and what it means for God's people."

"Then why are you here?" She pointed to the walls of her home. "This is not the Temple. Did the Lord *not* speak to you?"

Silence punctuated the air. The family of flies reentered the home and buzzed throughout the space, but no one spoke for a long time. Hilkiah cleared his throat. "The King told us that the Lord's

The Most Overwhelmed Women of the Bible

great anger is burning against us because our ancestors have not obeyed the words in this scroll. We have not been doing everything it says we must do."

"So you were frightened about what you would hear from the Lord directly—and came to me instead? Did you expect me to soften God's words?"

Hilkiah shook his head. "Please, if you know the word of the Lord, share it with us so we can relay it back to the King."

"Stand up," she told them.

They obeyed.

"This is what the Lord says." She pointed toward the Temple, then to the heavens. "I am going to bring disaster on this city and its people. All the words written in the scroll that the king of Judah has read will come true."

The men's faces registered shock.

She continued, knowing she must obey God rather than appease these officials. "For my people have abandoned me and offered sacrifices to pagan gods, and I am very angry with them for everything they have done. My anger will burn against this place, and it will not be quenched."

In the uncomfortable silence that followed, Hilkiah started to leave.

"Wait," she said. "There is more."

He batted away another fly. "Go on."

"But go to the king of Judah who sent you to seek the Lord and tell him this." She swallowed, tasting bile. "This is what the Lord, the God of Israel says concerning the message you have just heard: You were sorry and humbled yourself before the Lord when you heard what I said against this city and its people—that this land would be cursed and become desolate. You tore your clothing in despair and wept before me in repentance. And I have indeed heard you, says the Lord."

Hilkiah seemed to relax under the spell of these words.

"There is a bit more the Lord wants to say to Josiah," she said. She motioned for the five men to leave the house, and as they walked from the courtyard, she said these parting words from the Lord: "So I will not send the promised disaster until after you have died and been buried in peace. You will not see the disaster I am going to bring to this city."

The men left, promising to tell King Josiah the message from the Lord. Once they were out of sight, she allowed herself to sit on one of her chairs. She exhaled. There is a certain joy that comes when you do the right thing, even if it means pain for others. She thanked the Lord for entrusting her with this difficult message, then she took her now risen loaf outside to the oven and baked it until it browned.

The Biblical Narrative

The story of Huldah is found in 2 Kings 22:14–20 and 2 Chronicles 34:1–35 during the reign of King Josiah (641/640–610/609 BCE). Her name means "weasel." Rabbinic tradition says she was bestowed that name because she called King Josiah a man instead of The King. "Because of her haughty deportment, she was given a denigratory name, 'huldah,' meaning 'weasel' (even the Aramaic translation of her name—karkushta—sounds ugly)."[1] She was a contemporary of Jeremiah, Zephaniah, and Nahum.

To understand Huldah, we first must explore what the role of a prophet is in ancient Israel. A prophet is one who proclaims what they hear from God, irrespective of whether the audience wants to hear it or not. It's safe to say they are burdened with a message

80   The Most Overwhelmed Women of the Bible

that others may not want to hear. Prophets are often poetic—for instance, when you read the books of Isaiah or Jeremiah, you'll see the words in stanzas rather than blocks of narrative. Prophets chronicled history—as you see in both the major and minor prophetic books. They are also known as seers—as people who can supernaturally see the future, as revealed to them by God. They are typically devout and are attuned to the Lord. In other words, they long to hear from God, so they have a pious lifestyle and strive to be able to listen to God. Prophets speak the truth. They reveal God's ways and will to humankind. It was the prophet Samuel who codified the role of prophets, creating schools of prophets in his time. Before the time of Christ, prophets helped people find God.

A true prophet exhibited these traits. Amos 3:7 reminds us, "Indeed, the Sovereign Lord never does anything until he reveals his plans to his servants the prophets." Therefore, a prophet or prophetess is a servant, one who serves the Sovereign Lord.

A false prophet's attributes can easily be discerned by simply looking at the opposite traits of true prophets. Here are four simple truths:

- A true prophet speaks the truth he/she hears from God. A false prophet tells lies. (See Jeremiah 14:14).
- A true prophet's words come true. A false prophet's words do not. (See Deuteronomy 18:21–22).
- A true prophet does not shrink back from telling hard realities. A false prophet tells people what they want to hear. (See Jeremiah 28:5–9).
- A true prophet lives a godly, God-fearing, upstanding life. A false prophet lives an ungodly, pagan lifestyle. (See Jeremiah 23:9–16).

Huldah, the Burdened One

CBE International has a concise description of the female subset of prophets:

> The label "prophetess" or "woman prophet" (*něbî'āh*) is attributed to five women in the Old Testament: Miriam (Exod. 15:20), Deborah (Judg. 4:4), Huldah (2 Kings 22:14; 2 Chron. 34:22), Noadiah (Neh. 6:14), and "the prophetess" (Isa. 8:3). Its significance is clear. Miriam claims the Lord "has spoken" through her (Num. 12:2). Deborah says to Barak: "Look, the Lord, the God of Israel, has commanded" (Judg. 4:6). Huldah similarly uses the prophetic introductory formula: "Thus says the Lord God of Israel. . ." (2 Kings 22:15). Scripture, then, describes a woman prophet as someone through whom God speaks to his people. In this regard, a "prophetess" is no different than her male counterpart, the "prophet" (*nābî'*).[2]

It's interesting to note that although King Josiah explicitly told his five messengers to inquire of the Lord at the Temple, the narrative says they disobeyed that specific command and, instead, traveled to Huldah's home, which was in the northern extension of Jerusalem, a "suburb" of the Temple and palace that housed people who worked in both.[3] She used the common phraseology, "The Lord, the God of Israel, has spoken!" (2 Kings 22:15). Her prophecies both came true. (Jerusalem was captured; Josiah was spared.) She fulfills the true office of a prophetess.

Her message is both judgmental and salvific. She pronounces the oft-written judgment God promised the Israelites if they continued to pursue other gods. But she also said that Josiah would be saved from experiencing the fall of Jerusalem. The result of her

82   The Most Overwhelmed Women of the Bible

proclamations was Josiah's renewal of the covenant publicly when he read the Book of the Law in the Temple, vowing personally to keep God's ways, and asking the people of God to pledge themselves to the covenant. This culminated in a celebration of the Passover.

In early and middle church history, we see mentions of Huldah. She is mentioned in the Apostolic Constitutions. "Creator of man and woman, who filled Deborah, Anna, and Huldah with the Spirit . . . look upon our servant who is chosen for the ministry and grant your Holy Spirit."[4] John Knox wrote an apologetic for the role of women to John Calvin:

> There were occasionally women so endowed, that the singular good qualities which shone forth in them made it evident that they were raised up by divine authority; either that God designed by such examples to condemn the inactivity of men, or for the better setting forth his own glory. I brought forth Huldah and Deborah.[5]

Certainly, Huldah demonstrated great faith and bravery even as she was burdened with a message. She did not shirk from speaking the word of God to people in authority. She didn't cushion her words. The fact that she had words to share meant she spent time with God. That he used her meant she was a woman of godly character. Her words came true, which marks her as a true prophetess.

What Does This Mean for Overwhelmed You?

Stress from Wanting to Please Others

With such confidence seemingly exuding from Huldah, how might she be overwhelmed? The answer lies in the problems inherent to the life of a prophetess. While we may not have that specific gifting from the Lord (see a listing of spiritual gifts in Romans 12:6–8; 1 Corinthians 12:4–11, 28; and Ephesians 4:11), we all are stewards of the giftings God has given us. The question becomes: How does giftedness turn into overwhelm? What enabled Huldah to boldly operate within her area of gifting without shrinking back? And what kind of stress could she have faced?

I touched on this earlier, but Huldah certainly could've had a human desire to please people rather than her God, experiencing the strain between those two desires. In her time, the prophet Jeremiah condemned Hananiah the Seer who folded, giving in to the desires of the nation over the actual warnings God had given his true prophets. Hananiah prophesied that all would be well and their captivity in Babylon would be quickly reversed. Jeremiah sarcastically responded, "Amen! May your prophecies come true! I hope the Lord does everything you say. I hope he does bring back from Babylon the treasures of this Temple and all the captives" (Jeremiah 28:6). But then, like Huldah, he expresses the unpopular truth. "But listen now to the solemn words I speak to you in the presence of all these people" (28:7). He then tells Hananiah about his demise. "The Lord has not sent you, but the people believe your lies" (28:15), and then he prophecies his death. Two months later, Hananiah died. The pressure to bend to the opinions of others is always strong. In the New Testament, the Apostle Paul is quite black and white about how believers are to live. "Obviously, I'm not trying to win the approval of my people, but of God. If pleasing people were my goal, I would not be Christ's servant" (Galatians 1:10).

As a people-pleaser to my core, I have experienced a lot of overwhelming feelings when the desire to please God clashes with my hope for peace, particularly with a bully. My first reaction is not to seek God for his clarity, but to automatically apologize to keep the peace, even if I did nothing wrong. That, of course, harms me, but it also allows for another to be harmful toward another human being. Even recently, someone apologized to me in a blanket statement that did not really get at the specific, measured words they flung my way—words that had taken years to get over. What did I do? I offered forgiveness. I'm not saying we shouldn't offer forgiveness (of course we should). But what I'm trying to communicate is that sometimes we fail to honestly confront others because we are afraid of them and their opinion. We'd rather just appease.

In this world, it's quite easy to mimic and parrot the world's "wisdom," particularly on social media. Messages like "you are enough," or "just manifest your life," or "live your truth" permeate the zeitgeist of our world. It's easy to accept these happy messages because there is some small kernel of truth in them. But the reality is we aren't enough (God is); we can't make things happen (only God can); and no matter how much we want something to be true, it may be a lie. I believe God is raising up prophetic women who are willing to speak the truth without fear of a cultural hand-slapping (or canceling). It would have been quite easy for Huldah to capitulate to the desires of the nation's leadership to hear all is well and there would be no consequences to their years of practicing idolatry, but she chose instead to expose sin and share the heart of God with those in power.

The Pain of Telling the Truth

One of the most overwhelming periods of my life came when I advocated for sexual abuse victims within the Southern Baptist Convention. The toll it took on me was too much to write about, but suffice to say that I had to take a sabbatical after all that

Huldah, the Burdened One 85

advocacy. Why? Because the message I brought was unwanted and constantly pushed against. My words were certainly not popular, and I was attacked from without and within. But I felt compelled by the Lord to speak up for those who did not have a voice. Even though I knew this would be a painful process and journey, I did it. (Please don't think I'm brave. It was the Lord who impressed all this upon me, and I was simply obeying him. In my flesh, this is the last thing I would want to do, particularly as an avowed people-pleaser.)

There will come times in our lives when we face a forked road. On one path is the narrow way of speaking the unpopular truth, and the other is the broad, easy way that will merit the applause of many. In times like that, it's always good to memorize Acts 5:29, where Peter and the apostles are warned not to speak anymore in the name of Jesus. They respond, "We must obey God rather than any human authority." God's will trumps the will of the people. His ways are more important than our own comfort. His glory matters far more than our own. That is the pathway of discipleship, of choosing to do the hard thing, come what may.

The Overwhelm of Insecurity

There may also be a battle of insecurity when we're thrust onto a bigger stage. It used to be that we could be obscure (much like Huldah may have been), but today, everyone has a potential platform. Huldah instantly became public when the five men visited her home in search of God's will. The question became: Would she share God's message, even if it hurt? We now have that same opportunity, but perhaps we're wondering, *Who am I to speak into this?* Most likely, Huldah was laboring in quiet, being faithful in small things when this larger opportunity presented itself before her. She exemplifies the steward who was entrusted with five talents (see Matthew 25:14–30) and doubled her master's money. Her efforts were without fanfare; she simply did what was required of her. She emulated Jesus's words in Luke 17:10: "In the same way, when you obey me, you should say, 'We are unworthy servants who have simply done our duty.'" Telling the truth is a simple duty. Jesus elaborates on this quiet act of faithfulness when he says, "If you are faithful in little things, you will be faithful in large ones. But if you are dishonest in little things, you won't be honest with greater responsibilities" (Luke 16:10).

Stress from a Fickle Crowd

Something we face today is the fickleness of the Body of Christ to believe every wind of doctrine. People prefer to have their ears tickled to hearing the difficult truths of the Bible. Paul warns his disciple Timothy of this in 2 Timothy 4:3–4 when he writes, "For a time is coming when people will no longer listen to sound and wholesome teaching. They will follow their own desires and will look for teachers who will tell them whatever their itching ears want to hear. They will reject the truth and chase after myths." If we have a message that we feel compelled to share with the church, it may not be well received.

The Pain of a Broken World

Today's broken society is its own heavy burden. Huldah lived in a culture prone to idolatry, and ours is no different. Sometimes the sheer pressure of evil and debauchery causes us distress and overwhelm. I mentioned Jeremiah's words during the exile in chapter 29 in which he encouraged the remnant to seek the prosperity of the country in which they were living (Babylon). Theirs was a defiant joy of trusting the God of the universe while living in a

Huldah, the Burdened One 87

pagan nation. The first fear would be that the exiles would allow the nation to rub off on them, causing them to further sin. It's important that we evaluate ourselves to see if we are more like the culture around us or more like Christ. The prophet Ezekiel issues a warning when he writes, "Son of man, give the people of Israel this message: You are saying, 'Our sins are heavy upon us; we are wasting away! How can we survive?'" (Ezekiel 33:10). Then the prophet issues a warning: "As surely as I live, says the Sovereign Lord, I take no pleasure in the death of wicked people. I only want them to turn from their wicked ways so they can live. Turn! Turn from your wickedness, O people of Israel! Why should you die?" (Ezekiel 33:11).

When we're living among an unclean nation, we must remember to discern enough not to conform to its norms (see Romans 12:2). Instead, like Paul admonishes, we are to actively renew our minds so we can discern truth from error, right from wrong, God's wisdom versus humanity's wisdom. Jesus tells us to shine before others, and that light always consumes darkness. In short, we are to be different from the world around us.

But how? Peter gives amazing advice to believers living in difficult places:

> Now, who will want to harm you if you are eager to do good? But even if you suffer for doing what is right, God will reward you for it. So don't worry or be afraid of their threats. Instead, you must worship Christ as Lord of your life. And if someone asks about your hope as a believer, always be ready to explain it. But do this in a gentle and respectful way. Keep your conscience clear. Then if people speak against you, they will be ashamed when they see what a good life you live because you

88   The Most Overwhelmed Women of the Bible

belong to Christ. Remember, it is better to suffer for doing good, if that is what God wants, than to suffer for doing wrong! (1 Peter 3:13–17)

Look at the commands in this passage:

- Do right.
- Don't be afraid of threats.
- Worship Christ.
- Explain your faith, gently.
- Keep a clear conscience.
- Suffer for doing good, not wrong.

Friend, it's normal to feel overwhelmed by the wickedness of this world we live in. You're in good company—it also grieves the heart of God. No doubt it troubled Huldah too. But as you live your life, fearing God, confessing sin, and sharing your faith in a kind and gentle way, you are ushering in your little corner of God's ever-expanding kingdom. Don't give up. Remember the words of the Apostle Paul when he was facing persecution and discouragement:

That is why we never give up. Though our bodies are dying, our spirits are being renewed every day. For our present troubles are small and won't last very long. Yet they produce for us a glory that vastly outweighs them and will last forever! So we don't look at the troubles we can see now; rather, we fix our gaze on things that cannot be seen. For the things we see now will soon be gone, but the things we cannot see will last forever. (2 Corinthians 4:16–18)

Truths About Bold You

- It is possible to thrive in a perverse culture.
- Fearing people will prevent you from speaking/telling the truth.
- God will give you the courage necessary to speak the truth in love.
- Obedience in quiet places matters.
- Whether you're speaking to important people or plain ordinary folks, it's imperative you share the truth.

Questions for Discussion

1. What did you know about Huldah before picking up this book? What did you learn anew?
2. What did you uncover about the nation of Israel and how they acted prior to the exile?
3. What role did prophets and prophetesses play in the history of Israel? What role do they play (if any) in the church today?
4. When have you had a difficult message to bring to someone? What happened? How does Huldah's story encourage you?
5. What character traits did Huldah possess that you admire?

CHAPTER SIX

Esther, the Fearful One

Esther valued her cousin Mordecai's words—treasured them, actually. He had practically raised her, so when he approached her one day under the canopy of a happy sun, she embraced him.

"Hadassah," he said, then kissed both cheeks.

In hearing her given Hebrew name, she thrilled—an indication that he truly knew and loved her. "What is it, dear cousin?"

"You have no doubt heard of the demise of Queen Vashti."

She shifted out of the sun, sitting under the short roof canopy. Too much of the sun's kiss meant darkened skin. "Yes, she dared to defy him, I heard. And she paid quite a high price."

"Banished!" said Mordecai. "And she cannot be reinstated."

"Why is that?" Esther noticed Mordecai's sweat trickling down his cheeks. She fetched him an earthen cup of water.

He drank hungrily. "The Law of the Medes and the Persians is set up in such a way that when a decree is created, it cannot be revoked. Once a law is enacted, it is codified in rock and cannot be

92   The Most Overwhelmed Women of the Bible

unetched." He ran a rough hand over the foundation stone of their Susa home. "And that is why I am here. It seems another law has been enacted."

"Why does that concern me?"

Mordecai stood, pacing under the sweltering sun. For a long time, he said nothing. He cleared his throat of phlegm, spat, then looked at Esther. "There is an opportunity," he said.

She shook her head. Her cousin had always been shrewd, trying to provide for her any way he could. He knew how to wrangle and wrestle to gain favor and money in this exilic land. What scheme had he come up with now?

Before she could ask, he said, "King Xerxes's attendants sought to shift his anger from Vashti's defiance by distracting him. There is to be a search of the land, throughout all the provinces under his control for beautiful young virgins."

"What has that to do with me?" She fidgeted with her hands. Her stomach protested, something it did whenever she worried.

"You are beautiful, no?"

"I am simply a Jewess longing for home."

"And perhaps that is what makes you the most beautiful of all." He took her hands in his. "Hegai, the King Xerxes's eunuch in charge of the royal harem—he will be giving beauty treatments to the loveliest girls in the land. Then those women will be shown to King Xerxes. The one who most pleases him will become queen!"

"I don't understand. How does that concern me?" she asked, but she already knew the answer. She could read it in her cousin's eyes.

"You must become one of those women, dear Hadassah, but you must do so stealthily."

"I do not want to do this," she said. "Please."

"I believe this is a door opened for you by Almighty God. I cannot say why because I do not know myself, but please step forward. This is a rare, unprecedented opportunity for you to thrive and be provided for."

<hr>

Under Mordecai's strict warning, Esther did not tell a soul of her ethnic origin. Jews were disliked in this part of the world in the citadel of Susa, so she submitted herself quietly to a year's worth of beauty treatments, though her loneliness threatened to choke her. Her dear cousin must have known this because he, at great risk to himself, found a way to pace the courtyard beneath the king's harem to inquire about her. Sometimes he spoke to her directly, salving her sadness. She chose to submit to Hegai's instructions and potions, then asked him about his life, earning his kindness and favor. He told her he was impressed by her, and he asked if she'd prefer a different diet than the others. With joy, she said yes, and he obliged. He arranged for seven maids to attend to her and gave her the preferential spot in the harem among the other beautiful women. But the relentlessness of oils and perfumes and ointments weighed on her. Was she simply a woman of appearance? What did this external work profit?

She prayed each day, knowing that the night would come when she would be summoned like chattel to the bed of the king. Nerves wrecked her digestion—so much so that sometimes she forgot to eat. Esther had never been with a man, let alone a king. And this meeting would determine not only her destiny, but perhaps Mordecai's as well. So much pressure. So little choice. Though she despised her captivity and longed, alongside her exiled nation, to return to the confines of beautiful Jerusalem, she still held the Law of God within her heart. And God, may he be praised, intended for one man to marry one wife. So to be corralled with other women who would also be one with the king made her wary and afraid.

All she could do was treat her now-friend Hegai with compassion, listen to him, and bear his burdens. He and her attendants became her entire world, so she sought to bless them with *hesed* as God Almighty had blessed her.

She thought often of her mother, Abihail, who was the most beautiful woman in the world to her. Oh, how she longed to ask her advice, but the grave gave no such utterance.

"Today is the day," Hegai told her as she walked the pathway on the north side of the harem's walls.

"I am afraid," she said. And this was the truest truth. She felt it from her curled hair to her ankles.

"It will be for your favor," he said. "Do not worry. I have procured the best jewelry and clothing for you. You will stun King Xerxes in every way. I know it."

"I am stunned to silence. What will I say? What will I do? I know nothing of the ways of men, and certainly not of the demands of royalty."

"Be yourself—your lovely, beautiful self," Hegai said. He took her arm as they promenaded back toward the harem. "Let me prepare you for what is next because I know you like to understand the lay of the land before you step onto it."

"This is true," she said.

"This evening, you will be taken to the king's private quarters—where all the wives live. You'll be under the care of Shaashgaz."

"No! I don't want to leave you behind!"

"It is the way of things," Hegai said, taking her hand. "He is a eunuch as I am. He is safe, and I know him to be kind."

She didn't believe such words. Hegai had become a brother to her, nearly as precious as dear cousin Mordecai.

"One night, you will be summoned by the king."

Her stomach lurched.

"And if he prefers you, he will send for you again. I have hope that he will do that."

"I have no such hope," she said, allowing a tear to escape her left eye, layered with charcoal. There would be a streak of dark gray down her cheek now, she knew.

Nothing could quell the worry in her stomach. The king had called for her, and she told herself to focus on Hegai's words. Esther knew she could not rely on her own expertise.

"You look beautiful." Hegai adjusted her palla, robing her in a beautiful sky blue. He placed a floral crown on her head. Wafts of jasmine distracted her in the moment. "We do this as a subtle reminder that you are the queen he seeks."

Hegai stepped back. Looked at her. Smiled. "You will amaze him, dear Esther."

Part of her wanted to stay in that place—her home for a year surrounded by young women who had become her sisters. Hegai, of course, had brothered his way into her life in the best way. To leave meant saying goodbye to a life she enjoyed. What would the future hold? She prayed again to God, hoping he would not hold her accountable for what she had to do next. She was to become what she was not—alluring, demure.

The corridor seemed excessively long as she walked toward King Xerxes's quarters. Her gait became so slow that she could count the stones of the palace as she trudged there. Perhaps God would stop her, but no matter how slowly she walked, no such intervention came.

She neared the doorway that would lead her inward, away from her life. Esther swallowed. Prayed again. Remembered how Vashti had been humiliated because of the whim of a king.

Before she could knock, a man opened the door and greeted her. "I am Shaashgaz," he said.

"But I thought—"

"In due time. Didn't Hegai tell you that you would come here first? Before the king summons you?"

She let out a long breath. "Yes, he did. My mind has been on many things. I forgot."

He walked her down another long corridor and presented her new living quarters, familiarizing her with protocol and the rules of that place. Thankfully, many of the faces were familiar, and she embraced several women. She wanted to ask them what the king was like, but fear held her back.

⌘

In the seventh year of King Xerxes's reign, during the early dawn of winter, he summoned Esther. Though nervous and beyond frightened, she was surprised that the king wanted to talk with her, asking questions, and inquiring about who she was, what she liked. She was careful to not disclose her heritage, though she feared how she looked would give that away somehow.

But their meeting and connection had been convivial, and she startled when he touched her arm as she was leaving.

"You will be my queen," he told her. "And we will have a celebration—a public holiday to commemorate your coronation."

And it was so. What the king decreed happened. And to her delight and surprise, he appointed Cousin Mordecai to work as a palace official. Through the beautiful providence of God, she had become queen of a nation not her own. And he had provided proximity to dear Mordecai, who faithfully offered counsel and help whenever she needed it.

<hr />

"Esther, over here!"

Esther turned to see Mordecai, red-faced, behind a doorway. "What is it, cousin?"

"There is a plot to kill your king." He recounted the names and intentions of two of the king's men. "You must warn him." He put his fingers to his mouth as if to convey the quietness of the situation.

After she disclosed the plot, King Xerxes thanked Esther, who made sure to credit Mordecai with the intelligence. When his officials investigated the claims, they found them to be treacherously true and impaled the two men on a sharpened pole.

<hr />

Life continued for Esther as the favored queen, though she struggled at times to endure the rantings and ravings of King Xerxes's noble, Haman, who had taken to believing himself a god, demanding that everyone bow before him. She could not help but think Haman hated her, and she tried her best to avoid him. Of late, he had the king's ear over a matter she could not discern—what with officials running here and there issuing decrees and sending them all over the kingdom. She knew enough about kingdoms not to ask or intervene. Curiosity was not a valued trait in a queen.

98   The Most Overwhelmed Women of the Bible

A few days later, Shaashgaz approached her, his eyes downcast. He motioned for her to come into a private room. "I come bearing difficult news," he told her.

"Oh no," she said. "What could possibly be wrong?" She sat on the silk-lined couch. All she could think of was her only living relative. "Is Mordecai well?"

"He is not, Queen Esther."

"Is he sick?"

"He is not, but he may as well be. He wears sackcloth and goes about mourning and wailing at the castle gate. No one can console him."

"Does he say why?"

"No, he seems to have forgotten his words."

"He cannot stay in that state. The king—"

"Perhaps if you send him some new clothes, he will discard the mourning vestments and turn around."

So she sent new clothes immediately, but Shaashgaz returned just as quick, saying he would not accept them.

"Get me Hathach, please," she said.

When Hathach, one of the king's eunuchs, arrived she whispered, "You must ask Mordecai what is wrong. I must know!"

Far too much time passed as she paced the corridors and hallways of the palace, wearing a pathway of worry. Finally, Hathach returned. He handed her a scroll.

"What is this?"

"A decree from Susa that calls for the death of all the Jews."

"What?" Her heart raced. What could this mean? Why would the king do such a thing? In her mind, this could only be the work of Haman.

"Mordecai instructed me to tell you to go to the king to beg for mercy and plead for your people."

Esther stepped back. "So you know who I am?"

Hathach nodded. "But it is our secret."

For a long moment, neither of them spoke as the gravity of her predicament settled in on her. Finally, she said, "Tell this exact message to my cousin." She took a breath. "All the king's officials and even the people in the provinces know that anyone who appears before the king in his inner court without being invited is doomed to die unless the king holds out his gold scepter. And the king has not called for me to come to him for thirty days."

Hathach agreed.

Esther wished she didn't have to have all this clandestine conversation. Sending messages back and forth became excruciating, and her stomach certainly felt the weight of her precarious situation.

When Hathach returned, his countenance looked troubled. "I am afraid it's difficult news," he said.

"Just tell me plainly." Esther paced her quarters, then looked out the broad window facing King Xerxes's kingdom, her kingdom.

"Very well," he said. "Mordecai told me to tell you this: 'Don't think for a moment that because you're in the palace you will escape when all other Jews are killed. If you keep quiet at a time like this, deliverance and relief for the Jews will arise from some other place, but you and your relatives will die. Who knows if perhaps you were made queen for just such a time as this?'"

Sunlight danced on the tops of the trees. Birds sang melodies of joy. But the scene before her only soured her mood. What did beauty matter when such atrocities were afoot—and at the hand of her husband, no less? She swallowed, then turned toward Hathach, whose mood remained dim. "Tell my cousin this: Go and gather together all the Jews of Susa and fast for me. Do not eat or drink for three days, night or day. My maids and I will do the same. And then, though it is against the law, I will go in to see the king. If I must die, I must die."

It's an odd thing to think *today is the day I will die*. Most people don't have the luxury of that kind of knowledge. If they did, they would, perhaps, do something spectacular or world-changing. But despite the knowing, Esther's nerves would not allow any sort of benevolent effort. All she could do was instruct her maidens to dress her well. Her stomach no longer grumbled after three days of fasting—instead, her lack of hunger settled her, made her resolute. She could hear her footsteps echo down the courtyard as she approached the palace's inner courts, just across from the king's hall.

When she saw the king sitting on his royal throne, facing her, she gasped. There would be no way to cautiously approach him by stealth, as he caught her eye. In a moment, King Xerxes extended his royal, golden scepter her way. She should have been relieved, but in so many ways, this made her task more precarious.

She touched the scepter's end, as was the custom.

"What do you want, Queen Esther? What is your request? I give it to you, even if it is half the kingdom!"

She steadied herself, told herself to be as calm as the bluest sky. "If it please the king," she said, "let the king and Haman come today to a banquet I have prepared for the king."

The king smiled as if to say that was a reasonable request. He turned to one of his attendants. "Tell Haman to come quickly to a banquet, as Esther has requested."

After the bustling of preparing the banquet with her, when Haman entered the ballroom, she told herself to be calm. Even his presence far away made her nervous. She poured Haman and the king wine, hoping that this would sedate them, or at least keep their hearts merry.

King Xerxes took her hand, then looked her in the eyes. "Now tell me what you really want. What is your request? I will give it to you, even if it is half the kingdom!"

She would keep his gaze, not venturing it away in case she caught the hard stare of proud Haman. "This is my request and deepest wish. If I have found favor with the king, and if it pleases the king to grant my request and do what I ask, please come with Haman tomorrow to the banquet I will prepare for you. Then I will explain what this is all about."

<hr />

From her window she noticed a large pole being erected by Haman's men. Its top was meant to impale, she knew. Was Haman speeding up his murderous plot?

But wind of another plan came to her through Hathach. "May I approach, my lady?" he asked.

"Of course, particularly if you bring news of today's commotion!"

He recounted that the king had a restless night, then passed his insomniac time by reading through the history of his ruling. There, he uncovered Mordecai's valiant information. He asked an attendant what the palace had done to recognize Mordecai, but the attendant said nothing had been done. "And as it happened, Haman was in the king's courtyard at that very moment. The king beckoned him, then asked Haman, 'What should I do to honor a man who truly pleases me?'"

The Most Overwhelmed Women of the Bible

Esther could see God's poetic justice being spun before her. "And did he think this honoring was for himself?"

"Yes, and he had been the one creating an impaling pole for Mordecai, so the irony was thick," Hathach said.

"What did Haman say?" She moved closer to Hathach, arms on her knees.

"Well, you can imagine," the eunuch said. "But the details are these: the honoree should wear the king's royal robes, ride a royal horse, and an official would lead the person through the city square, shouting, 'This is what the king does for someone he wishes to honor!'"

"And this happened today to Mordecai, and Haman had to say those words?" She wondered why she had not yet heard of it.

"Yes, and now the king's eunuchs are bringing Haman your way for the banquet."

Esther steadied herself as she entered the banquet hall. Her words deeply mattered, as did her mannerisms. This delicate situation worried her, and the weight of her people felt heavy upon her heart.

Thankfully, the king motioned for others to listen, which they did. Not a sound could be found, though moments ago boisterous conversations had echoed off the stone walls. "Tell me what you want, Queen Esther," he said. "What is your request? I will give it to you, even if it is half the kingdom!"

She swallowed and felt the courage of Cousin Mordecai and the history of her people well up within her. "If I have found favor with the king, and it if pleases the king to grant my request, I ask that my life and the lives of my people will be spared." She paused, looking at Haman, whose charcoal eyes seared into her. "For my people and I have been sold to those who would kill, slaughter, and annihilate us. If we had merely been sold as slaves, I could remain quiet, for that would be too trivial a matter to warrant disturbing the king."

The King grunted. "Who would do such a thing?" He slammed his chalice on the table. Wine poured onto the floor, dripping like blood. "Who would be so presumptuous as to touch you?"

Courage empowered her to look at Haman again. "The wicked Haman is our adversary and our enemy." She watched as the cocky man morphed from prideful to meek.

The king jumped to his feet, rage in his eyes. He left the banquet hall and ran into the garden adjacent to the palace.

Part of her wanted to follow the king, but God's presence kept her there.

Haman's despair escalated before her. He begged her to spare his life, but she said nothing, pretending as if he were an errant mosquito. He dared to approach her, then fell prostrate on her couch. She moved away from him, horrified.

Just then, the king returned, fire behind his eyes.

She motioned at Haman.

The king's face reddened, never a good omen. "Will he even assault the queen right here in the palace, before my very eyes?"

Without a word, the king's servants knew exactly what he meant. They covered Haman's face with a cloth. Everyone there knew what that would mean. Certain death.

Harbona, another of the king's eunuchs, approached King Xerxes. He bowed. The king extended his scepter toward him. "Haman has set up a sharpened pole that stands seventy-five feet tall in his own courtyard. He intended to use it to impale Mordecai, the man who saved the king from assassination."

"Then impale Haman on it!" the king ordered.

Though a decree could not be reversed once enacted, the king did send Mordecai's words to the 127 provinces that gave the Jews permission to fight back, sealed by his signet ring. This decree empowered the Jewish people to defend themselves against attack. In this victory, Queen Esther, along with Mordecai, established the Festival of Purim to celebrate such a great deliverance.

The Biblical Narrative

The Book of Esther takes place between Ezra 1–6 and Ezra 7–10, after the first wave of exiles returned to Jerusalem, as well as after the Temple was rebuilt. She is clearly living as an exile in the Persian empire (particularly Susa), with 127 districts under the reign of Xerxes, the son of Darius. Susa is situated in modern-day Iran; it's where Nehemiah served as Darius's cupbearer. You can read more about this time in Ezra, Daniel, and Haggai. The Book of Esther is famously known for *not* mentioning the name of God, though his provision, deliverance, and fingerprints are all over the narrative.

Perhaps the most-held belief by scholars is that the Book of Esther points toward God's providence. The famous preacher Charles Haddon Spurgeon elaborates, "It is his joy to perceive that the Lord is working according to His will in heaven, and earth, and in all deep places. It has been well said that the Book of Esther is a record of wonders without a miracle, and therefore, though equally revealing the glory of the Lord, it sets it forth in another fashion from that which is displayed in the overthrow of Pharaoh by miraculous power."[1] We see deliverance and God's rescue, which, I would argue, is miraculous, even if no sea was parted.

Esther has two names: Hadassah, which means myrtle, and Esther, which means star. She is an orphan who is taken in benevolently by her uncle Mordecai, and the text clearly indicates that she loves and

Esther, the Fearful One   105

respects him, seeks his advice, and obeys his words. In many ways, he is a father to her. She trusts him and chooses to go along with his plan for her to "audition" for the queenly role. After a year of beauty treatments, she is taken to the king in December or January in 478 BCE. The word used to describe the king's favor toward her is *chen*, which is found six times in this book. It's the same word in Genesis 6:8: "But Noah found *favor* with the Lord" (emphasis mine).[2]

Haman, on the other hand, has a name that means magnificent, which is what he tends to think of himself. He personifies Proverbs 6:16–19: "There are six things the Lord hates—no, seven things he detests: haughty eyes, a lying tongue, hands that kill the innocent, a heart that plots evil, feet that race to do wrong, a false witness who pours out lies, a person who sows discord in a family." He is a man after praise and glory, and he has a fueled hatred for the Jews—particularly Mordecai, whose relationship with the One True God will not allow him to bow before another man. Haman, however, had much favor with the king because he seems to persuade the king easily to annihilate the Jews. Another indication of his extreme pride comes in Esther 5:11, when he shared with his wife and friends "and boasted to them about his great wealth and his many children. He bragged about the honors the king had given him and how he had been promoted over all the other nobles and officials."

In the aftermath of Xerxes's declaration, Mordecai's lament is loud and unrelenting, so much so that word reaches an alarmed Esther. He is the one, through Hathach, who acts as a proxy, who utters the most famous words of the Book of Esther: "If you keep quiet at a time like this, deliverance and relief for the Jews will arise from some other place, but you and your relatives will die. Who knows if perhaps you were made queen for such a time as this?" (Esther 4:14). Mordecai's faith is so strong that he believes even if Esther does not intervene, God will find another way to rescue his

106   The Most Overwhelmed Women of the Bible

people. But his words also echo the tenuousness of Esther's situation. Where she sits, she is endowed with privilege and responsibility.

The pivotal declaration of this book comes with Esther's response: "And then, though it is against the law, I will go in to see the king. If I must die, I must die" (Esther 4:16b). Hers is a similar declaration to Jacob's when he instructs his sons to return to Joseph in Egypt, come what may. "May God Almighty give you mercy as you go before the man, so that he will release Simeon and let Benjamin return. But if I must lose my children, so be it" (Genesis 43:14). There comes a point when we must place all things in God's hands, come what may. And all we can do is step out and trust that he will do good on our behalf.

Throughout this book, as mentioned earlier, you see the providential hand of God. God enables Mordecai to uncover a plot to kill the king. He keeps the king awake at night so that he'll remember Mordecai's good deeds precisely before Haman comes to visit (and then misunderstands the king's intentions). We see the poetic justice of Haman being forced to praise his enemy, Mordecai. And we see the king's extension of kindness toward Esther on two distinct occasions. The plan unfolds perfectly. Justice is meted out on the very impaling pole meant to destroy a loyal Jew.

But to get there, Esther had to demonstrate uncanny bravery, and her overwhelm must've been extreme. By approaching Xerxes, she was breaking a law, one that could end in her death. She also had to publicly admit she was a Jew, something she had hidden from him their entire relationship. This points to her being a deceiver, and, therefore, treacherous. She had to somehow convince a proud king to see his legislation as wrong. It's interesting to note that the king had procured a lot of money (billions in our currency) to carry out this order. To reverse it or change course meant a large economic loss, not to mention loss of power if he allowed such a reversal.

One of the things I noticed was a familiar phraseology used by Xerxes that is also found in the New Testament. He said to Esther, "What is your request? I will give it to you, even if it's half the kingdom!" (Esther 7:2). Later, we see these words coming from King Herod's mouth, but the outcome is not salvation, but annihilation. His wife's daughter Herodias (who shared the name with her mother) danced before him. "'Ask me for anything you like,' the king said to the girl, 'and I will give it to you.' He even vowed, 'I will give you whatever you ask, up to half my kingdom!'" (Mark 6:22–23). After consulting with her mom (who detested John the Baptist), she asked for his head. In the first instance, a wife intervened for the lives of many; in the second, a wife orchestrated the death of one.

In the end, Esther's bravery is part of God's plan to save the Jewish people from certain death. She is far more than simply a beautiful bride. Throughout her time in the king's palace, you see her garnering favor, making relationships, and respecting people, particularly the king. She exists within the confines of her life in Persia. But she is not a passive player on God's stage. Her risk of her own life reveals a deep-seated faith and a compassion for others.

We can also draw many parallels between Esther and Jesus:

- She was placed in her position of power before deliverance was necessary. Similarly, we see Jesus in the place of redemption even prior to creation. "They are the ones whose names were not written in the Book of Life that belongs to the Lamb who was slaughtered before the world was made" (Revelation 13:8b).
- Esther fasted three days prior to facing death, and it was during the Passover feast. Jesus celebrated the Passover feast, and his death would follow.

108 The Most Overwhelmed Women of the Bible

- Esther was clothed in royal robes prior to facing a possible execution. And for Jesus? "They dressed him in a purple robe, and they wove thorn branches into a crown and put it on his head" (Matthew 15:17).
- Esther entered the throne room. Jesus entered the most holy place. "With his own blood—not the blood of goats and calves—he entered the Most Holy Place once for all time and secured our redemption forever" (Hebrews 9:12).
- Esther's act brought non-Jewish people to Judaism. "In every province and city, wherever the king's decree arrived, the Jews rejoiced and had a great celebration and declared a public festival and holiday. *And many of the people of the land became Jews themselves*, for they feared what the Jews might do to them" (Esther 8:17, emphasis mine). Jesus grafted in the Gentiles as he built his church. "For Christ himself has brought peace to us. He united Jews and Gentiles into one people when, in his own body on the cross, he broke down the wall of hostility that separated us. He did this by ending the system of law with its commandments and regulations. He made peace between Jews and Gentiles by creating in himself one new people from the two groups" (Ephesians 2:14–15).[3]

What Does This Mean for Overwhelmed You?

God Is Sovereign

Perhaps the most important lesson for those of us who are overwhelmed is remembering the sovereignty of God and our response to that character trait. A sovereign is a ruler (see the root word *reign*), like a king is sovereign over his kingdom. Sovereignty, then, is the "rulingness" of God, his ability to perform perfectly as the King of the universe. While it is easy for me to understand that a sovereign ruler rules well in matters of a realm, it's harder for me to personalize it, to see his rule and reign in my life. Our sovereign God is personal, after all. Job understood this. At the end of his experience with the God of the universe who asked him questions he could not answer, he declared, "I know that you can do anything, and no one can stop you" (Job 42:2). We live in the tension of God's sovereignty, we who have wills and free wills. It is both practicality and mystery. In Proverbs 16:33, we see this tandem truth of our culpability and his reign. "We may throw the dice, but the Lord determines how they fall."

One of the most comprehensive passages about God's rule comes from the Prophet Isaiah:

> "I create the light and make the darkness. I send good times and bad times. I, the LORD, am the one who does these things. Open up, O heavens, and pour out your righteousness. Let the earth open wide so salvation and righteousness can sprout up together. I, the LORD, created them. What sorrow awaits those who argue with their Creator. Does a clay pot argue with its maker? Does the clay dispute with the one who shapes it, saying, 'Stop, you're doing it wrong!' Does the pot exclaim, 'How clumsy can you be?'" (Isaiah 45:7–9)

Here we clearly see God as the creator of everything, and we are his creatures. His purposes will prevail. Just as Job hollered back at God when horrible circumstances prevailed upon him, we can

The Most Overwhelmed Women of the Bible

do the same—but according to Isaiah, we are pots arguing with the potter.

In the New Testament, one of my favorite passages about God's sovereign rule is in Colossians 1:16–17: "For through him God created everything in the heavenly realms and on earth. He made the things we can see and the things we can't see—such as thrones, kingdoms, rulers, and authorities in the unseen world. Everything was created through him and for him. He existed before anything else, and he holds all creation together." Not only does God rule, but he rules because he created everything he rules over. That last part is quite important—the God of the universe holds everything together. That snippet of a verse has held me through times of tumult. In so many ways, he has held me together when overwhelm threatened to drown me.

As I look back on my life, particularly those times when I was exceptionally overwrought by my circumstances, I can now see God's hand in them. Our current overwhelm can cloud our vision, but as we grow in Christ, we learn the art of reminding ourselves of God's sovereign ability to work in and through difficult circumstances. There's never been a moment in time when I said something to the effect of, "Wow, I really grew in Christ when my life was full of ease." It's only been through the trials and pains that I've seen him do his deepest work and his most surprising deliverance. As we trace Esther's life, we see this working through her pain—and we also see the sweetness of God. Though an orphan, she was adopted by a kindhearted relative. Though in a harem, she became queen. Though she dared to ask the king for a favor (which wasn't allowed), he extended the scepter her way. Though she was scheduled to be annihilated, she was not only allowed to live, but she incurred favor.

Others Are Watching

Another fascinating thing we can learn from the story of Esther is that even when you don't feel seen, people are watching and taking notice of your faithfulness. We see this in the interaction between Esther and Hathach the eunuch in Esther 4. He witnesses the entire plotline of the possible Jewish destruction. And he sees how God capably handles the situation.

Two of the most profound times of growth (and heartache) in my life happened during the end of two of my close friends' lives. And, interestingly, they were best friends. Twila battled cancer for several years, and Shelly was her right-hand girl, researching treatments for the impossible cancer she faced. It was Twila who taught my husband and me how to come back to life after our time as missionaries in France. She is the one who basically forced us (in the most Twila-based hysterical way) to start a Life Group at our church when what we really wanted to do was hide. She saw our potential, even as we were broken. It was not long after that when she received the diagnosis. She lived her life to the fullest, and she became an example of godly suffering to us. If there's ever a way to grow through someone else's pain, I believe we experienced that. In other words, her faithfulness fueled us, made us want to live better lives, and drew us closer to Jesus.

After Twila's death, Shelly faced her own terrible diagnosis. We watched as cancer ravaged her body, but it could not take her love for Jesus. We accompanied her to have the elders of our church (of which my husband was one) lay hands on her and pray. We ate with her, prayed with her, and laughed with her. We had a back seat (and often a front seat) in watching her suffer well. Truly, Shelly's grace in the face of death changed me fundamentally. When I face the specter of death, hers is the example I'll remember. We learn far more by life-learning than we do by book-learning, after all. And Shelly's life was the most profound classroom.

If you're in that state of overwhelm, be encouraged. People are watching. You are providing others with a tutorial on how to suffer. Paul reminded the Corinthian believers to "imitate me, just as I imitate Christ" (1 Corinthians 11:1). And he gives that same kind of mandate to his disciple Timothy. "Don't let anyone think less of you because you are young. Be an example to all believers in what you say, in the way you live, in your love, your faith, and your purity. Until I get there, focus on reading the Scriptures to the church, encouraging the believers, and teaching them" (1 Timothy 4:12–13). Whether we like it or not, God has given us the privilege of living our lives before others as examples. I felt this more keenly when my children were younger. I understood that they would learn far more by my demonstration of the gospel more than my articulation of it. How I treated their dad mattered. How I handled conflict would be how they would deal with it. How I persevered through trials could become a blueprint for them later on.

By writing this, I'm not intending to put pressure on you. No one can suffer well without the help of the Holy Spirit and others. No one can be a perfect specimen under the microscope of inspection. But the truth is that we are being watched. And as I think about Twila and Shelly, I believe some of their greatest kingdom work came when they were at their weakest. Perhaps yours will, too. I believe they could utter Paul's powerful words, "As for me, my life has already been poured out as an offering to God. The time of my death is near. I have fought the good fight, I have finished the race, and I have remained faithful" (2 Timothy 4:6–7). In the midst of overwhelm, how you make your way through matters. I know the race is long, and it's often a slog. I have been in that place of utter overwhelm, asking when-oh-when will this stop. But I have also encountered the

Esther, the Fearful One   113

truth of Zechariah 4:6: "It is not by force nor by strength, but by my Spirit." It's the very Spirit of God who loves to do his best work through our weakness. As you look back on the story of Esther, there are many points in the story where she shares her inadequacy and fear. She is brave not because she lacks fear, but because she is riddled with it and still chooses to trust in the strength God provided her.

Esther's overwhelm was intense, but it did not persist forever. Peter offers encouragement about the brevity of overwhelm when he writes, "In his kindness God called you to share in his eternal glory by means of Christ Jesus. So after you have suffered a little while, he will restore, support, and strengthen you, and he will place you on a firm foundation" (1 Peter 5:10). We are told that the present sufferings we face in this world are temporary (see 2 Corinthians 4:17 and the surrounding context). They will not compare with the glory that is our inheritance. When I'm amid overwhelming circumstances, I try to remind myself that this trial is brief in the schematic of the universe. It is a blip, a single point in a long line reaching eternally.

When No One Is Watching

But there are times of suffering where we truly feel no one is watching. No one is learning from our supposed faithfulness. Suffering feels relentless and arbitrary, and there is no horizon that beckons an ending. That's where theology matters. Because the truth is that the Lord sees you. Psalm 56:8 encourages us: "You keep track of all my sorrows. You have collected all my tears in your bottle. You have recorded each one in your book." Nothing is unnoticed under the all-seeing watch of the One who collects your tears. While that may feel like thin reassurance, knowing that nothing escapes God's notice can be tremendously encouraging. Consider these promises from Psalm 139:

- God knows everything about you (vs. 1).
- God knows your every action, every thought (vs. 2).
- God knows your travel schedule and your homebody days (vs. 3).
- God knows every word you're about to say (vs. 4).
- God goes before you; he follows after you; as he does, he blesses you (vs. 5).
- God is with you when you face the grave (vs. 8).
- God is with you when you move around the earth (vss. 9–10).
- God is near in the darkest of days (vss. 11–12).
- God created you (vss. 13–15).
- God has ordained your days (vs. 16).
- God constantly thinks about you (vs. 17).
- God is with you when you awaken this morning (vs. 18).

As we learned from the book of Esther, God is sovereign. But he is also intimately acquainted with us. When we are overwhelmed, he is not. When we are brokenhearted, he is near. When we feel alone, he is alongside us. When we lived in France as missionaries, I felt so very alone—crushed by loneliness, actually. But there were moments when I would wake up in the middle of the night, sad and afraid, where I would sense his "withness." Like he did with Esther, he sent intervention, people, and surprising deliverances, but the sweetest part of all that suffering was his nearness. The verse I had memorized in college became my cry: "But as for me the nearness of God is good for me; I have made the Lord GOD my refuge, so that I may tell of all your works" (Psalm 73:28 NASB). That's my prayer for you as you continue reading this book about overwhelm. May you instead be overwhelmed with the nearness of God!

Truths About Brave You

- When you feel like life is out of control, your sovereign God holds all things together.
- Courage is not the absence of fretting; it's the presence of it while still moving forward.
- Your witness may simply be enduring trials well.
- God's deliverance often comes in unexpected ways.
- When you're overwhelmed, it gives God a chance to be the strength in your weakness.

Questions for Discussion

1. How has Esther been traditionally portrayed? How did reading this account change your perspective of her?
2. How would you feel in Esther's situation (in the harem, when she had to risk her life)?
3. Look up the Festival of Purim. What do you learn about God's character through the way people traditionally celebrate it?
4. List all the circumstances Esther could have felt overwhelmed about. How do those differ from your current struggles? How are they similar? What can you learn from her?
5. What political changes have taken place since Esther's experience? What has remained the same?

CHAPTER SEVEN

Elizabeth, the Barren One

Elizabeth spent the day waiting in her hill country village, busying herself with the tasks of her life. She could not put words to why this day loomed differently. On the surface, all seemed to be normal in her corner of Judea. Her husband, Zechariah, a priest in the order of Abijah, performed his priestly duties in the Temple. She heard from others (as she was too frail to make the journey herself) that Zechariah drew the lot to enter God's beautiful sanctuary. He would burn incense as instructed. Today a crowd would be praying, their words echoing the ascending fragrance.

How many times had he faithfully served the Lord in that place? And how many of their prayers had gone unanswered? Too many to count. She swept the earthen floor, attempting to dispel the dust from her mind. Mornings were always harder these days.

Quiet.

A few birds sang melodies in a distant orchard, but there was no cadence of children's trilling in earshot. There had never been.

The Most Overwhelmed Women of the Bible

And there would never be—as her age had reminded her constantly. Aching joints meant a slow morning while she sipped hot tea slowly. Still, she prayed. She asked God to empower her to be faithful in her home, to love the people in her circle of life, to bless Zechariah.

Later in the day, she heard the strange report.

"Zechariah tarried in the Temple," their neighbor Joshua told her. "He spent more time in there than anyone before him."

"Why do you suppose that is?" she asked, offering him water.

He took a long drink, then thanked her. "He can no longer speak."

She pressed him for further details—like was Zechariah sick? Did he suffer a malady therein?

Joshua shook his head. "I am sorry. I do not know. Some say that perhaps he saw a vision."

After his week of Temple service came to an end, Zechariah returned to her, mute. She embraced him, then pulled away. His eyes sparkled, as if they held a delicious, yet holy secret.

Soon, she grabbed a slate, and he began to write. He communicated that an angel frightened him, but that the supernatural being had a message for Zechariah and Elizabeth. She would conceive, have a son, and his name would be John. He would be a Nazirite, refraining from wine and strong drink—and he would be full of God's Spirit, even before he entered the world from the womb. He would be a prophet, turning the nation toward God. He would wear Elijah's mantle, and he would be a forerunner, a man who prepared people for the coming Lord. Fathers would return home to their children. Rebels would repent.

Elizabeth, the Barren One   119

It was far too much to digest. Elizabeth shook her head. "But why can't you speak, dear Zechariah?"

He scribbled, *The angel's name is Gabriel, and he told me that because I didn't believe right away, I would be mute until our child is born. He said that I could be assured that his prophetic words would come true.*

The throwing up came a few weeks later, and with that, a deep knowing that the God who created everything from nothing opened a barren womb. Elizabeth marveled. Often, like Zechariah, she had no words to describe how she felt, so she quietly pondered the mysteries of God. But one morning, she blurted, "How kind the Lord is! He has taken away my disgrace of having no children." The moment she said it, she remembered the words of Tamar, David's daughter who lamented, "Where could I get rid of my disgrace?" Only she bore the weight of her disgrace for the rest of her life. Why would God change Elizabeth's circumstances so radically? She had no response other than gratitude.

She touched no wine, and she prayed often for this "John" who had been endowed with an important task. But what did Gabriel mean when he said he would be filled with the very Spirit of God before he was even born?

For five months she remained in seclusion, cherishing this undeniable miracle kicking against her ribcage. Perhaps because she had longed for so many years, then grew accustomed to the reality of childlessness, she cherished these moments more keenly.

In her sixth month as she showed a swollen belly to the village, her cousin Mary entered her home (it was a surprise to see her!).

The Most Overwhelmed Women of the Bible

The moment Mary said hello, then kissed her cheek, baby John leapt within her, nearly dancing. At that precise leap, a warm presence engulfed her, full of a familiar peace. She remembered her husband's words on the tablet, that the baby would be filled with God's Spirit prior to birth, and she marveled. Why was God so good that he would not only bless her child with such power, but also pour his presence over her? At once, a knowing came over her—something she could not have perceived by merely looking at her cousin. Mary was with child—and that child would be the deliverer they were longing for. She touched each of Mary's shoulders and looked into her eyes. "God has blessed you above all women, and your child is blessed," she heard herself say.

Tears erupted in Mary's eyes. "It is as the angel said!"

"What do you mean?" Elizabeth asked.

"Just that I already knew you were with child, even before I made my very long journey! You are a confirmation of miracles—astounding feats only God could do."

"But it is I who am witnessing his greatness again," Elizabeth replied. "Why am I so honored, that the mother of my Lord should visit me? When I heard your greeting, the baby in my womb jumped for joy."

Mary embraced her.

Eventually, she pulled away and looked Mary in the eyes. "You are blessed because you believed that the Lord would do what he said." Again, these words were not her own—it was as if the God who opened wombs were uttering encouragement through her.

It was then that Mary's tongue unleashed in ecstatic, poetic, melodic praise.

She sang:

Elizabeth, the Barren One

"Oh, how my soul praises the Lord.
How my spirit rejoices in God my Savior!
For he took notice of his lowly servant girl,
and from now on all generations will call me blessed.
For the Mighty One is holy,
and he has done great things for me.
He shows mercy from generation to generation
to all who fear him.
His mighty arm has done tremendous things!
He has scattered the proud and haughty ones.
He has brought down princes from their thrones
and exalted the humble.
He has filled the hungry with good things
and sent the rich away with empty hands.
He has helped his servant Israel
and remembered to be merciful.
For he made this promise to our ancestors,
to Abraham and his children forever."

"Stay with us," Elizabeth encouraged.

Mary agreed.

Elizabeth knew the stigma her unmarried cousin bore, and she knew it was her job to protect and honor her. It was only later that she heard Mary's story with the same angel, Gabriel, who told her she would carry the son of God, conceived of the Holy Spirit. Only Mary still had her voice—as she received that declaration without any wavering of belief. Zechariah honored Mary for such a thing, as he now regretted his doubt before the angel.

Their time together—an old woman bearing an impossible son and a young cousin bearing an even more impossible one—went fast. They treasured each moment, recounting the goodness of God to choose lowly people like themselves—unknown to many, but known to God and visited by angels.

Mary's departure was bittersweet. It was time for Elizabeth to give birth, and they both somehow knew it was time for Mary to return to her home. They cried upon each other's shoulders, determined to pray for their upcoming births, and promised to stay in touch.

"Zechariah," she whispered. Though her husband uttered no words, he slept like the dead, complete with snoring. He did not rouse. She shook him. Nothing. Finally, she shouted his name, and he sat upright. The light of the moon shone through their window well. "It is time," she said.

He fetched a midwife, then stepped outside.

The contraction of her abdomen happened at regular intervals now, and each one felt as if Goliath himself gripped her. She cried out to God. She cried out to Zechariah. She squeezed the midwife helper's hand, tears pouring down her cheeks. They were tears of pain mingled with tears of absolute joy. Old Elizabeth would be pushing a new life into the world.

"It is time, Elizabeth. Take the deepest breath, then push harder than you ever have."

She obeyed the midwife's encouragement and yelled her way through her bearing down.

In a moment, she experienced release and relief, the pain immediately gone.

And with that, the most beautiful cry—robust, strong, ready.

"It's a boy," Elizabeth said.

"How did you know? I have not yet told you."

"I know."

On day eight, Zechariah made preparations for the baby's circumcision ceremony while Elizabeth recovered. She was grateful for a husband who was so kind. Many from their village gathered. One of the village elders asked to hold their baby, and she handed the swaddled boy his way.

"Ah," the old man said, "What a handsome boy you are, young Zechariah!"

"No," Elizabeth said. "His name is John!"

"What?" the elder asked. "There is no one in all your family by that name." He looked away from her, as if her voice had no merit, then motioned for Zechariah to settle this ridiculous matter. Of course the baby would be named after his father.

Zechariah gestured for a writing tablet, which Elizabeth gave him. He wrote, "His name is John." And then he spoke! For the first time in ten months, he shouted "Hallelujah!"

The old man's eyes widened. He handed the baby back to Elizabeth. She took note of the gasps of shock and looks of surprise—a delight she had quietly lived these past nine months. Now her village was experiencing the entirety of the miracle alongside her. At first, she could not quite retrieve the words to describe the moment, but later she said it was a holy awe. The story would spread throughout the hill country of this mute man, his aged wife, and a baby with a strange name.

The elder asked, "What will this child turn out to be?"

Zechariah responded in poetic praise:

The Most Overwhelmed Women of the Bible

"Praise the Lord, the God of Israel,
because he has visited and redeemed his people.
He has sent us a mighty Savior
from the royal line of his servant David,
just as he promised
through his holy prophets long ago.
Now we will be saved from our enemies
and from all who hate us.
He has been merciful to our ancestors
by remembering his sacred covenant—
the covenant he swore with an oath
to our ancestor Abraham.
We have been rescued from our enemies
so we can serve God without fear,
in holiness and righteousness
for as long as we live."

He took baby John, newly circumcised and crying, and said:

"And you, my little son,
will be called the prophet of the Most High,
because you will prepare the way for the Lord.
You will tell his people how to find salvation
through forgiveness of their sins.
Because of God's tender mercy,
the morning light from heaven is about to break upon us,
to give light to those who sit in darkness and
in the shadow of death,
and to guide us to the path of peace."

Elizabeth let Zechariah's words be her own. She knew all these things—about Mary's baby in her womb, and baby John who now

Elizabeth, the Barren One

whimpered. She took him gently from Zechariah, cooed over him, looked in his eyes, and marveled at all the Lord would someday do through him.

The Biblical Narrative

We only read this story of Elizabeth, Zechariah, and John's birth in the Gospel of Luke. Doctor Luke writes his letter to Theophilus, whose name means loved by God. Scholars disagree about whether this is an actual person or a name for a general believer who is loved by God. Sometimes you'll see the two books written together as Luke-Acts because Luke authored both books. Luke is a chronicler, one who meticulously attends to details. Perhaps that is why his gospel contains Elizabeth's story. The first two verses of chapter one are these: "Many have undertaken to draw up an account of the things that have been fulfilled among us, just as they were handed down to us by those who from the first were eyewitnesses and servants of the word." Those words "draw up" comprise the word *anatassomai*, which means to arrange in a row. When you read the Book of Luke, you are getting a play-by-play narrative, first things first. Which is why the birth of John the Baptist, who plays an important role in the life of Jesus, is chronicled first. That Luke used eyewitness accounts means he most likely spoke with either Elizabeth or Zechariah or both.

To understand the context of this story, we must unpack the political history of Judea. Herod the Great ruled (but these events took place toward the end of his reign). He was not a Jew. He was known to have had nine or ten wives, one of which he had executed. While he had expanded the Temple, he placed a Roman eagle over its entrance, and he also erected idolatrous temples. He did what was best for him—he was no friend of the Jewish people. He also was the same ruler who infamously had the young boys

126   The Most Overwhelmed Women of the Bible

massacred around the time of Jesus's birth (see Matthew 2:1–2). He ruled from 37 BCE to 4 BCE.[1]

The Jewish people had endured four hundred years of God's silence, and the Old Testament Book of Malachi recorded the last words they heard. Malachi had prophesied the coming of Elijah: "Look, I am sending you the prophet Elijah before the great and dreadful day of the LORD arrives. His preaching will turn the hearts of fathers to their children, and the hearts of children to their fathers. Otherwise I will come and strike the land with a curse" (Malachi 4:5–6). Can you hear the echoes of Malachi's words in Gabriel's declaration? "He will be a man with the spirit and power of Elijah. He will prepare the people for the coming of the Lord. He will turn the hearts of the fathers to their children, and he will cause those who are rebellious to accept the wisdom of the godly" (Luke 1:17). Before you pass judgment on Zechariah, consider how radical these words are! He, as a priest, would have known Malachi's prophecy. How could his old, barren wife bear one who was like the prophet Elijah? This certainly was something difficult to wrap one's mind around.

The questions people asked at the time were these: *Where is God? And does he care about our plight under the mighty fist of Rome?* They were looking for a political messiah to free them from the tyranny of a foreign oppressor.

Into this setting, we see Zechariah, a priest of God. As Philip W. Comfort noted in *The Life Application New Testament Commentary*, "At this time there were about twenty thousand priests throughout the country. Priests were divided into twenty-four separate groups of about one thousand each (1 Chronicles 24:3–19). Zechariah was a member of the order (or division) of Abijah. Each division served in the Jerusalem Temple twice each year for one week."[2] Elizabeth, too, came from the line of Aaron—a priestly lineage. Having two people from the same priestly lineage was a

Elizabeth, the Barren One

surprising blessing. According to the text, they were both righteous, but they had no offspring. This is a strange contradiction because barrenness often meant (in that culture) that you were cursed by God, or you must have done something wrong to deserve that state, although Luke makes no such conclusion.

Even so, we see an echo of what Jesus would do later when he met and healed the man born blind. He said, "This happened so the power of God could be seen in him" (John 9:3b). And we also see this later in the death of Lazarus: "Lazarus's sickness will not end in death. No, it happened for the glory of God so that the Son of God will receive glory from this" (John 11:4). Taken in this context, Elizabeth's age and barrenness were impossible situations—except for God. His glory shines through impossibilities. And, in the context of the scope of this book, he overwhelms the overwhelmed with his redemption.

When Mary visits Elizabeth, she makes quite a trek, from Nazareth to the hill country—a trip estimated between fifty to over seventy miles.[3] When the two pregnant women greeted each other, the word used in the Greek is *aspazomai*, which means to embrace, welcome, or enfold in arms.[4] When the baby within her (John the Baptist) "met" Jesus, he leaped (*skirtao*), which has the connotation of an animal bounding or springing or skipping about. The verb is only used one other time in the New Testament: "What blessings await you when people hate you and exclude you and mock you and curse you as evil because you follow the Son of Man. When that happens, be happy! Yes, *leap* for joy! For a great reward awaits you in heaven. And remember, their ancestors treated the ancient prophets that same way" (Luke 6:22–23, emphasis mine). How interesting that this second leap comes after many of the consequences John the Baptist encountered!

We see Elizabeth loudly proclaiming a blessing upon her cousin Mary. The word, *anaphoneo*, is used only this time in the New Testament. Her words are an eruption from within her, where the

128   The Most Overwhelmed Women of the Bible

Spirit of God shouts through her. In the overwhelm of turning from barren to bearing, then meeting the mother of the Lord of the Universe, her only reaction could be profound praise. The word for blessing here should ring a bell: *eulogeo*, from which we get the word eulogy, which literally means a good word.

After their time together of three months passes, Mary returns to her home, and Elizabeth gives birth to a son, John, who would be known as John the Baptist. When Elizabeth speaks his name publicly and Zechariah confirms it on the tablet, the priest suddenly regains his ability to speak. As a result, "awe fell upon the whole neighborhood, and the news of what happened spread throughout the Judean hills" (Luke 1:65). The word for awe here is *phobos*, which, as you may have guessed, means fear. The NET commentary says, "Fear is the emotion that comes when one recognizes something unusual, even supernatural, has taken place."[5] We see the supernatural, utterly powerful hand of God throughout Elizabeth's story that begins with deprivation (barrenness) and ends in praise and fear of God's great abilities.

Another parallel can be drawn between Elizabeth, who bore John the Baptist, and Manoah's wife, who bore Samson: Both boys who were Nazirites full of vigor ended up spending themselves for the nation of Israel. Imagine the overwhelm of both mothers when their sons sacrificed themselves for their people, both a foreshadowing of Jesus, who would do that once and for all.

What Does This Mean for Overwhelmed You?

Fear of an Uncertain Future

We have tackled the issue of barrenness and its link to overwhelm earlier in this book. But let's look at Elizabeth's unique situation. How might she be overwhelmed? She is most likely past childbearing age. The Scripture says "Zechariah and Elizabeth were righteous

Elizabeth, the Barren One 129

in God's eyes, careful to obey all of the Lord's commandments and regulations. They had no children because Elizabeth was unable to conceive, and they were both very old" (Luke 1:6–7). To have no heir and to be old was an economic crisis. Who would take care of her or Zechariah if they needed care?

There is much overwhelm today in these concerns—even if we do have children. Aging is not for the faint of heart. There is mystery to it and the very real possibility of personal decline. And then there are those of us in the in-between stages, where we are tasked with taking care of our own parents. Without children, Zechariah and Elizabeth faced their own uncertain future. But many of us, though we are surrounded by family, are often one medical emergency away from financial disaster.

When Religion Doesn't Work

Besides that, perhaps Elizabeth felt the overwhelm of her religion not working out for her the way she may have imagined. Though Luke says she was righteous, her state of barrenness could possibly indicate otherwise—was God judging her by keeping her barren? How many of us have asked questions like, "Lord, I have served you my whole life, so why haven't you answered this persistent, painful prayer?" or "Lord, why do I continue to face this relentless hardship?" Perhaps we are like the Apostle Paul, who begged God to remove a thorn, only to have God decline that earnest petition (see 2 Corinthians 12). This life in Christ is not a formula of doing all the right things to be guaranteed happiness and all our prayers answered in the way we want them to be. There is far more mystery to God's ways, coupled with the very evil world we live in that pushes against our joy.

Disappointment with God

Our overwhelm, then, can stem from our disappointment with God. When he doesn't "obey" our expectations, we can either sit in that sadness and let it marinate (eventually) into bitterness, or we can rightly grieve (which takes some time) and move through our frustration. Thankfully, we are not alone in this struggle. Most of the Psalms represent various psalmists crying out to the God who doesn't always act in the way they wanted him to. Reading the lament Psalms is instructive here. (See Psalms 3–10, 13, and 25 for a sampling.)

What I have learned in my own disappointment journey is this: God can "take" our anger. He welcomes our questions. That's a normative part of a healthy relationship to be able to freely ask questions, get angry, work through difficulties and misunderstandings, and find each other through the pain. It's entirely normal to be overwhelmed with our situations, particularly the ones that we have asked God to change. Currently, I'm walking through a season of bewilderment, not understanding why God is walking me down a path with an aging loved one. It's convoluted, confusing, and maddening, and it's bringing up all my past wounds. I've learned it's better if I'm simply honest with God in prayer, letting him know I'm disappointed in the way things have worked out. When I do that, my angst lessens significantly. If I stuff those emotions, I've learned that I'll probably have to revisit them later.

The Beauty of Not Comparing

When we are overwhelmed, we tend to compare our stories to others' stories rather than practice contentment with our own. Elizabeth did not do this. She rejoiced in another's fortune (Mary). Elizabeth experienced a supernatural occurrence—a divine intervention—but it was not as spectacular as Mary's. Mary met Gabriel. Mary's pregnancy came via supernatural impregnation. How did Elizabeth respond? With maturity and rejoicing. She exemplified Romans 12:15: "Be happy with those who are happy, and weep with those who weep."

Elizabeth, the Barren One   131

It's perhaps the strongest indicator of maturity when we can genuinely rejoice with someone else's win. And in doing that, we realize afresh that the kingdom of God is not a competitive entity—when another person wins, we all celebrate because it means the kingdom is expanding. If you find yourself automatically turning toward jealousy at another's seeming success, ask the Lord to reframe the situation from a lacking mindset to an abundance one—where there is plenty of joy for everyone, to move from worry toward seeking God's kingdom first. Jesus said, "So don't worry about these things, saying, 'What will we eat? What will we drink? What will we wear?' These things dominate the thoughts of unbelievers, but your heavenly Father already knows all your needs. Seek the Kingdom of God above all else, and live righteously, and he will give you everything you need" (Matthew 6:31–33).

We Need Each Other

In the case of Mary encountering Elizabeth, another truth emerges. God often relieves our overwhelm by the sending of a saint. Paul recounts an excessively difficult experience in which God intervenes with a person in 2 Corinthians 7:5–6. "When we arrived in Macedonia, there was no rest for us. We faced conflict from every direction, with battles on the outside and fear on the inside. But God, who encourages those who are discouraged, encouraged us by the arrival of Titus." Paul was unafraid to admit his overwhelmed state—he was honest and unashamed to be so. And God's beautiful solution was a person: Titus.

As I write this chapter, I am feeling the sting of conflict from all sides, battles aplenty, and so much fear that I need to talk myself down from panic. And in the middle of that, the Lord saw fit to encourage me through my German friend Tabea. I had reached out for prayer because the day bordered on overwhelm. She wrote,

"Been praying for you before the email came. Asking for prayer is the humble thing to do, I believe. We should all get better at it, so thanks for the modelling. Love you!" It was such a simple note, but it helped turn the tide of my day.

And perhaps that's the simplest lesson we can learn from Elizabeth's story: God uses others to bring refreshment and joy—and sometimes those others mean us. Blessing other people when we are overwhelmed may turn our stress around because it takes our eyes off ourselves and places them upon the needs of others. The question becomes: How can our lives and the way we conduct them give other people an opportunity to worship God? How can we become for someone else what we need?

God Can Be Trusted

The name Elizabeth means "God keeps his oaths." When we are overwhelmed, we must trust in the character and "oaths" of God, even when everything seems impossible. Throughout the Bible, we learn God is patient with us, seeks after us, hears our prayers, and is near to us when we're brokenhearted. He keeps his promises. With decades of infertility, Elizabeth continued to be righteous in God's eyes. She did not let go of her faith. And, in the end, God intervened in a surprising way. But even if he doesn't answer our prayer according to our will, it is still true that God is trustworthy, kind, and gentle. His ways are mysterious, but he is always good.

Nearsightedness

When we face overwhelm, we can become myopic. We may only see a small portion of our lives—particularly that part that brings stress. The problems we face loom large, and God shrinks smaller. It's imperative that we retrain our minds to move from natural to supernatural thinking. God *can* do the impossible. One of the verses that helps me reframe a gigantic struggle is Jeremiah 32:17: "O Sovereign LORD! You made the heavens and earth by your strong hand and powerful arm. Nothing is too hard for you!" In Elizabeth's case, God's strong and powerful arm did the impossible—he opened an empty womb. Later, he would open an empty tomb! The entire gospel is shrouded in the supernatural!

The Best Overwhelm

I would be remiss if I didn't mention a different kind of overwhelm as it pertains to the story of Elizabeth—being overwhelmed in a good way. There are moments in our walk with Christ—mountaintop experiences—when we are overcome by the goodness of God. He answered a prayer I had prayed for decades recently—and my overwhelm felt more like awe. For days I lived stunned, surprised, and grateful. While I would always prefer to see spectacular answers to prayer every day, I must thank God for the journey he took me on. I wouldn't have the maturity I have now had I not toiled and cried out (and despaired) in this journey of prayer. And all the roadblocks and heartaches along the way only augmented the sweetness of the answer. I scarcely have words for it right now.

Truths About Filled You

- Sometimes God intervenes supernaturally in a long-term situation or prayer.
- We can grieve our situation and, at the same time, be grateful for God's work in another's life.
- We have a choice to be faithful to God even when he doesn't answer our cries on our timetable.
- God often sends people to help us when we're overwhelmed.
- God can do the miraculous.

The Most Overwhelmed Women of the Bible

Questions for Discussion

1. How does the story of Elizabeth teach you about the character of God?
2. Have you experienced infertility or walked alongside someone who has? What have you learned?
3. How does the interaction between Elizabeth and Mary reveal the best traits of friendship?
4. What longstanding prayer request has brought heartache your way? How has God been answering that prayer over the years?
5. Who in your life truly rejoices when you have a win? Who do you love to celebrate with?

CHAPTER EIGHT

Mary, the Pierced One

Mary loved her God. Her heart thrummed with the rhythm of his ways. But at her young age, she knew there was much to learn about his character. When she was betrothed to Joseph, her first thought was, *His eyes are kind.* And her second? *We can serve the Lord together.*

She stood outside under a blessedly open sky, her back tired from sowing seeds, the edge of Nazareth's boundaries just below her as the sun opened its eyes in the east, casting shadows on her family's land. No one kept her company when she did this work—but she preferred it that way. Here, she could pray. And listen. And plan for the future.

A rustle of music flourished around her, startling her quiet morning. She turned to see a giant looming over her, his countenance radiant. He neither smiled nor frowned. The word she would later use was *resolute.* She looked behind her toward home, but the day remained as it had been, normal and quiet. Before she could speak, he motioned as if to silence her.

"Greetings, favored woman! The Lord is with you!"

What does this mean? Who is this? What is this? What is happening? Still, no questions left her lips. Anchored to the earth, she stood—a statue in the field.

"Don't be afraid, Mary." The music that had once filled the air now faded under the power of his voice.

How does he know my name?

"For you have found favor with God!" His words boomed, then echoed.

What could this mean?

Light continued to swirl around him, dust motes dancing in its illumination. "You will conceive and give birth to a son, and you will name him Jesus. He will be very great and will be called the Son of the Most High. The Lord God will give him the throne of his ancestor David. And he will reign over Israel forever; his Kingdom will never end!"

So many weighted words. What is this being saying? She pulled in a breath, then let it out. All she could think to ask was, "But how can this happen? I am a virgin."

The dance of dust faded, and light pooled at her feet.

The angel, as she now came to believe he was, nodded her way. "The Holy Spirit will come upon you, and the power of the Most High will overshadow you."

None of this makes sense.

"So the baby to be born will be holy, and he will be called the Son of God."

The prophecies of the Promised One.

"What's more," the angel said, "your relative Elizabeth has become pregnant in her old age! People used to say she was barren, but she has conceived a son and is now in her sixth month. For the word of God will never fail."

For a long moment, she said nothing. Her? A mother without consummating with a husband? The son of God? Her cousin with a child in her old age? All these miracles could only be the work of a God who had been silent four centuries. Though so much of it made little sense, one thing she knew: God was visiting his people, and he was using her to bring about this holy visitation. "I am the Lord's servant," she finally said. "May everything you have said about me come true." But even as she said those words of faith, her heart felt pierced, as if it were struggling to beat.

At Mary's declaration of the word *true*, the swirl of music intensified. The light, too. And as quickly as he had appeared, the angel disappeared, leaving her to ponder on what she just experienced. She pinched her arm, eliminating the possibility that this had been a dream, but the pinch hurt, and the sun kept rising, and her heart kept beating.

That evening, sleep evaded Mary. Her mind kept retracing the words of the angelic being—she would be overshadowed by the Lord God Almighty, and this would cause her pregnancy. She prayed, asking God how she should share this impossible and improbable prophecy with Joseph. Surely, he would think her mad, making up fantastical stories. She had always been known as an intelligent girl with a strong imagination—but this? How could it be anything but true? An angel from the heavenly realm had revealed all this to her, a messenger of what would happen. She thought of all the visitations of old—how angels foretold children who would deliver her people. The parallels were uncanny.

Mary placed her hands upon her stomach, wondering. Though the implications of an unwed pregnancy pummeled her mind, she also allowed herself to cherish this moment.

The night waned. Stars poked holes in the night sky and seemed to shine all the brighter—and as they did, sleep came. When she awoke, a strange warmth cocooned her, as if she were being held, comforted, and healed all at once. As the sun rose to the level of her window well, she chose not to arise, basking in the presence of God.

Before long, doubts began to creep into her mind, particularly when she worked in the same field where she had encountered the angel. "Forgive me, Lord," she said to the warming air, "but I need confirmation." In that moment, she knew: She must visit Elizabeth. If her elderly cousin was with child, she would know the angel's words would be confirmed.

Her parents granted the journey, though with many caveats and warnings. It would take her over four days on foot to do such a trek, and through difficult territory. As of yet, she did not tell them about her visitation, but her pleas were pointed and emphatic.

"Stay with family along the way," Mother told her. "Don't be ambitious—but stop when dusk appears."

"Yes, Mother," she said. "I will be careful."

Father handed her his walking stick. "In case you grow weary." A tear formed in one eye, then leaked down his beard.

As she walked that first day, the Sea of Galilee flanking her on the left, she made melody in her heart to the God of the impossible. Though normally full of vigor, particularly at her young age, she found the afternoon sapping her of strength. And as she stopped to

Mary, the Pierced One

refill her skin of water, a sudden pang erupted from her stomach. In a moment, she threw up her breakfast on the banks of the sea.

When she finally made it to the hill country, her fatigue on day four was so overwhelming that she nearly stopped in the middle of a pathway and lay in the dust for an afternoon nap, but Mary pressed on. And when she saw the humble home of Elizabeth and Zechariah, she nearly yelped with joy.

Before entering, she remembered the words of the angel, how the impossible was possible with her cousin. She wondered if everything had been a fanciful imagination. But as she entered her cousin's house, she saw the miracle—Elizabeth's bulging belly.

Elizabeth cried out with joy. She laughed, then cradled her belly. "God has blessed you above all women, and your child is blessed," she exclaimed.

My child? Is it true? Mary remembered her tangible-presence-of-God moment with God days earlier.

Elizabeth grasped both her hands. "When I heard your greeting, the baby in my womb jumped for joy. You are blessed because you believed that the Lord would do what he said."

Then it is true. All of it.

Mary could only respond with a song of praise, recounting God's mighty ways and his notice of such a lowly person as herself. That song became the welcome mat for an extended visit—three months to be exact—as her own belly began to swell.

Joseph had initially wanted to quietly separate from her for the sake of propriety, but the angel who visited him changed all that—which was something she treasured in her heart. Joseph would marry her, but they would not consummate their relationship as her belly grew.

For him to suffer embarrassment and shame alongside her made her young love grow. And that they both had encounters with heavenly visitors kept her guessing what God would do next. Joseph had descended from royalty, King David to be exact, and she shared that same lineage. Though she felt small, she marveled at how God had woven their two stories together to create a new King. A King of kings.

"We must go to Bethlehem," Joseph told her, kindness creasing his eyes.

"I am too much with child," she said, holding her belly. "That is a long journey."

Joseph took her hand. "Caesar Augustus has issued a binding decree—a census—and we are required to register in our ancestral towns. I am so sorry."

She sighed. Phantom pains now became more familiar with her, and fear ruled her heart with this declaration. Would she give birth on a dirt path? Would she survive? How could she make such a long journey?

"I have use of a donkey," he said, as if that solved everything.

Their journey slogged through Galilee, Nazareth growing smaller as she looked back. The constriction of her stomach came at more regular intervals. Mary told her body to hold that baby inside. And of course she prayed. She knew this baby was to be a deliverer—the question became her quest: Would God empower her to deliver such a one?

They finally neared the hillside of Bethlehem as dusk inked the day. So worn out, she lay backward on the donkey, looking up at the cobalt sky.

Mary, the Pierced One

Joseph had told her to wait—he would find lodging for them.

"Hurry," she had told him.

The contractions came in waves of anguishing pain. Mary squinted her eyes, telling herself to bear up under the agony.

"I have found a place."

She startled at Joseph's words.

"It is not ideal, but it is dry and somewhat warm." He led her on the donkey toward a rock-hewn stable. Mooing echoed through the dim space.

"Here?" she asked, her voice weakened.

He helped her off the donkey, then onto a bed of straw. He who had never known a woman caught the baby as she pushed him into the night air. "Jesus," he said.

A sheep bleated back.

Exhausted, she fell asleep, the boy cradled in a manger once she swaddled him well. But a group of men interrupted her rest. The stench from the animals matched the scent of the shepherds. One came forward, his earth-stained hands clasped together. "We saw something—amazing," he told them. "A host of angelic beings in the sky over our flocks, full of light, as if lightning was brightening the sky, only there were no clouds."

"Angels?" she asked. She thought of the angel she met, the angel in Joseph's dream, and now a group of angels. Surely this was confirmation of God's redemptive plan!

"Yes, ma'am. At first it was just one angel. He said, 'Don't be afraid.'" The shepherd shook his head, pulling on his beard. The other shepherds around him chimed in, demonstrating that they were indeed afraid. "The angel told us he brought us good news that would bring great joy to all people."

Good news. After four hundred years of God's silence, they certainly needed good news, she thought.

The man continued. "He said a savior, the Messiah, the Lord, has been born today here in Bethlehem. He even told us what we would find as confirmation."

Joseph came closer to the shepherd. "And what was that?"

The shepherd pointed to Jesus sleeping in the animal trough. "He said we would find a baby wrapped in cloth, swaddled in a manger. And then a whole army of angels joined the first angel and praised God in concert, giving him glory."

As they paid homage to her sleeping son, Mary treasured these words in her heart, wondering what it would mean for baby Jesus. She nursed him in the wee morning hours, noting the contour of his nose, his gentle sighs, and the way his right hand gripped her left index finger.

Forty days later, she and Joseph, poor and unable to afford a lamb sacrifice, thanked the Good Lord for the provision in the Law of giving turtledoves as an offering. Every firstborn male should be dedicated, and this special child was no exception. An older man called Simeon held Jesus and said he could die now that he laid eyes on the glory of Israel. He was joined by a prophetess named Anna who praised God for the infant. But it was Simeon's last words that haunted Mary. "And a sword will pierce your very soul."

Mary braced herself under the darkening sky, her heart wrenching. Her dear and beautiful son, her firstborn, bled from his head, hands, and feet at Golgotha. Her life felt tied to his, so much so that as he faced death, she felt certain she would die beneath him. The Deliverer had been delivered to the leaders of her people, who then delivered him into the hands of the Romans, their arch enemies. She could scarcely breathe as she watched him gulp in breath. If she

Mary, the Pierced One

could, she would be his lungs, but she could not ascend the cross and take his place. Nor could she be pierced in hands and feet or wear a twisted crown of thorns.

Memories came flooding in, then in rapid succession.

When the men of the East offered gifts to Jesus, costly gifts fit for a King—a King they discovered under a surprisingly bright star.

How their small family fled to Egypt under Herod's maniacal mandate to kill all the baby boys of Jerusalem.

How, before the death of her husband, God led them out of Egypt toward Judea, but an angel's warning directed them home to Nazareth.

When Jesus stayed behind in Jerusalem at twelve years old, and they found him talking high theology with learned scribes and teachers. His matter-of-fact retort that of course he would be in his father's house.

When, as a man, she watched when he turned water into miraculous wine—the color of the blood that wept down his face right now.

When he dismissed her, how he called everyone his father, brother, sister, and mother, giving her no special office. Oh, how her heart ached then. But it broke with a sense of knowing, that being a mother to a Messiah meant a relinquishment to his fate.

Miracles upon miracles—the deaf hearing, the blind seeing, the demon-possessed liberated, the leprous cured, the lame dancing, the broken made whole. His words about love, his affection for his disciples, his stories that perplexed so many. Words about a different kind of kingdom. Parables of truth. The entry earlier that week into a Jerusalem that stoned and killed its prophets.

Mary had no words, only gut-piercing grief, as she watched her son choke as he pushed up from his nail-spiked hands and feet. Crucifixion was the barbaric penalty for criminals, but Jesus had done nothing wrong—and now each breath could be his last. Simeon's long-ago words about her pierced heart were being fulfilled before her eyes. To her right wept her sister, Clopas's wife Mary, and Mary of Magdala—a crowd of broken witnesses to the horror. To her left stood John, whom Jesus had loved unto death. All held hands.

They said nothing.

And then Jesus caught her gaze from bloodied eyes. "Dear woman, here is your son." His gaze shifted to John beside her. She understood his instructions.

"Here is your mother," he croaked.

Even in death, Jesus chose to shepherd, to protect. But though she wanted to, she could not return the kindness. All she could do was stand there helpless while evil people hurled insults his way and wagered for his clothing—all while her heart ripped in two.

"I am thirsty," he said.

Someone beneath the three crosses hoisted a hyssop branch with a sponge to his lips, but he did not drink.

The darkening day blackened in that moment. No birds sang. What had been warm now blew cold, as if the weather was mourning. Mary prayed for her son, remembering all the angelic promises about him, all the marvels, all the miracles—to end in such an undignified way. A king? How could a king endure such torture?

"It is finished," Jesus shouted into the agonizing quiet.

His breath rattled out, but he took no further gulp of air.

Mary's heart wrenched. All was finished.

Only a savior could conquer death. Only a redeemer could dance out of a rich man's tomb. Only the Son of Man could vanquish such an enemy as the grave. Mary lived with John now, while the remaining disciples obeyed the mandate of angels—that the Jesus who ascended into heaven after his beautiful resurrection would send his Holy Spirit to them all.

So they waited.

And prayed.

And tarried.

And hoped.

Together, over a hundred of his followers, witnesses to the resurrection of their King, interceded in a cramped upper room in Jerusalem. Her son James prayed alongside them, too.

Peter, who had denied Jesus thrice, now stood emboldened before them. They attended to the office Judas left behind and cast lots for Matthias.

Day in, day out, they waited in expectation.

On the Day of Pentecost, the Festival of Firstfruits, Mary detangled all her memories—all those treasured moments she was now able to string together in a chronology of kingship. Jesus fulfilled so many prophecies. His miracles confirmed his deity. His immaculate conception made it so. And all those countless works—she knew they could not be chronicled. But now what? As the group of followers continued to gather and pray and talk, expectation lit up the room.

A rush of wind blew through the room of Galileans, as if the walls had become torrential clouds, but this wind was not a squall, but an embrace that hearkened Mary back to that moment so many years ago when she woke up held by the Almighty. She said, "Jesus."

Flames that did not consume—were they like the bush that beckoned Moses?—alit on each person's head. In a rush of time, Mary spoke a foreign language. She did not know what words she said, but they were intelligible, and somehow, she knew those strung-together syllables were utterances of praise to God, who was

146   The Most Overwhelmed Women of the Bible

now visiting them. Joy arose from within the group. Laughter too. And holy fear. And boisterous proclamation.

To her left, she heard an Egyptian dialect, one she partially mastered with her son and husband in Egypt. "God is great, and he does wonders. Blessed be his name!" How could the unlearned man next to her speak this way?

Mary thought back to the words the angel of God had told her. "Greetings, favored woman! The Lord is with you!"

He had been.

And he would continue to be.

She would spend herself for him for the rest of her life.

The Biblical Narrative

We see the story of Mary the mother of Jesus primarily in Luke 1–3, Matthew 1–2, John 2, John 19, and Acts 2. She plays a prominent role in the gospel narratives. Scholar Kelley Mathews writes, "She is the fourth-most mentioned New Testament character after Jesus, Peter, and Paul. And she, more than any disciple, consistently points people to her Son."[1] As we studied earlier, her story begins in the middle of Elizabeth's experience with barrenness, angelic visitations, and pregnancy. When Gabriel visits her, she is perplexed by his greeting, "Greetings, favored woman! The Lord is with you!" In the Latin Vulgate, these words should sound familiar: "Ave Maria," which means "Hail, Mary." The word "favored" is the common Greek word *charis*, which simply means "unmerited favor." In other words, she did nothing to earn the distinction of Mary the Mother of Jesus. This was a sheer gift. And what a gift it was!

This gift was prophesied about in the middle of a particularly dire time in Israel's history when Ahaz (the grandson of Uzziah) was facing a Syrian attack. It's important to remember that prophecy

Mary, the Pierced One

has a telescoping aspect to it. In other words, the prophetic words are often for that moment, a moment in the future, and a moment in the far, far future. In this prophecy, the Lord tells Ahaz that the impeding attack will never occur. Then Isaiah the prophet tells him, "All right then, the Lord himself will give you the sign. Look! The virgin will conceive a child! She will give birth to a son and will call him Immanuel (which means 'God with us')" (Isaiah 7:14). In Ahaz's time, though, a virgin did not conceive. This pointed forward to a time when a deliverer would come for Israel through supernatural means. And God would use a young woman whose heart bent toward his purposes.

There are surprising parallels in Luke 1 between Gabriel's visit to Zechariah and his visit to Mary. This is known as a *synkrisis*, "a comparison, which invites us to complete the two."[2] Both were troubled by their angelic visitations. Both were told not to be afraid. Both were foretold a son (though one, John the Baptist, would come through natural means, while Jesus would come through supernatural means). Both were told what to name this son. The angel foretold those sons' potential greatness. The difference is that Zechariah didn't exercise belief, but Mary did. She was a woman of faith, one who dared to believe the impossible.

In looking at Gabriel's words I mentioned earlier, "Greetings, favored woman! The Lord is with you" (Luke 1:28), we hear echoes of Judges 6, when Gideon is also visited by an angel. "Mighty hero, the Lord is with you!" In doing so, we see a strong connection with the nation of Israel's difficult history and its need for a deliverer. Gideon supernaturally delivered the Israelites; Mary's offspring would supernaturally deliver all humankind.

When we read (frequently) that Mary "kept all these things in her heart and thought about them often," we often remember the phraseology in the NIV: "treasured up." That word "treasured,"

148   The Most Overwhelmed Women of the Bible

suntereo, is in the imperfect tense. That means it's a continual action. The "thought about them often" verb is *sumballo*, which means to reflect on something deeply—in the moment. So Mary is a woman of contemplation and deep thinking.

Another parallel we see is the language Luke uses when pointing toward waiting for the Holy Spirit, both for Mary and for the emerging, embryonic church. "The angel replied, 'The Holy Spirit *will come upon you*, and the power of the Most High will overshadow you. So the baby to born will be holy, and he will be called the Son of God'" (Luke 1:35, emphasis mine). Here, she is to wait for the power of the Holy Spirit. Later, a resurrected Jesus tells the disciples, "And now I will send the Holy Spirit, just as my Father promised. But stay here in the city until the Holy Spirit *comes* and fills you with power from heaven" (Luke 24:49, emphasis mine). Before Jesus ascended to the Father, he used the same language: "But you will receive power when the Holy Spirit *comes upon* you. And you will be my witnesses, telling people about me everywhere—in Jerusalem, throughout Judea, in Samaria, and to the ends of the earth" (Acts 1:8, emphasis mine). The Greek word used in Luke 1 and Acts 1 for "come upon" is *eperhchomai*, and "power" is the same as well: *dunamis*. *Eperchomai* means to "supervene, i.e. arrive, occur, impend, attack, (figuratively) influence: come (in, upon)."[3] *Dunamis* simply means "power." So, we see the Spirit coming upon Mary with the conception of Jesus, and we see the same thing (as she is in the Upper Room) when the church is conceived. How beautiful and interesting that Mary was present at both occasions—the Mother of the Lord and a mother at the onset of the church.

As you probably know, Mary and I share the same name. It's the same name Naomi converts to when she's bereft of sons and husband: *Mara*, which means bitter. Taken into the context of the narrative of Jesus's life, this makes sense. Like Naomi, Mary most

Mary, the Pierced One

likely experienced the death of Joseph, as he is not mentioned in the narratives when Jesus is an adult and has started his ministry. And then to watch her firstborn, dedicated-to-God, Messiah son be crucified like a criminal—I can think of no other thing that would embitter a mother more.

Imagine what it would feel like to watch your child, the one you bore, agonize to breathe, pushing up on nail-pierced hands and feet in order not to suffocate. Imagine what it would feel like to hear untrue accusations hurled his way. Imagine how you would feel if people mocked your child, feigning worship, but ridiculing instead. How would you feel if your child told the Father to forgive those who crucified him? Crucifixion is humiliating, excruciating, and exposing (they were crucified naked). And in the middle of this utter turmoil, your son makes provision for you—telling John to take you in, provide for you. The condescension of Jesus in that moment is poetic and profound. He is said to have loved the disciples "during his ministry on earth, and now he loved them to the very end" (John 13:1b). But here, he loves another one of his disciples, his mother Mary, to the very, very end by providing for her.

Whole books have been written about Mary, and I feel inadequate to address every nuance here. But suffice to say, we often do her a disservice by diminishing her because our Catholic friends nearly deify her. There is so much to her life that is commendable and follow-able. From the Magnificat, we see a woman who knows the Scriptures and her place in God's plan. From her response to the angel's puzzling proclamation, we see someone who is perplexed, but faithful. She is someone who contributed humanity's DNA in Jesus's hypostatic union, fully human, fully divine. We see a prophetic woman who understands the nature of the gospel before it is even preached (See Luke 1:46–55, particularly, "He has filled the hungry with good things and sent the rich away with empty hands" vs. 53). She fulfilled the Law in having Jesus circumcised, then dedi-cating Jesus in the Temple, though she and Joseph were poor and could only offer birds (rather than a lamb). Although only men were required at the Passover, year after year, Luke reminds us that the whole family, including Mary, ventured to Jerusalem yearly, reveal-ing her devout praxis. Mary understood her son's capabilities at the wedding in Cana and witnessed his very first recorded miracle. She is the longest disciple, connected to Jesus from the beginning of his life and his ministry, and she moved to Capernaum to be near him. And she was present at his death when many deserted him. She was a faithful follower who was deeply overwhelmed, but also completely faithful.

What Does This Mean for Overwhelmed You?

Ordinary Person in Complicated Circumstances

Mary played a significant role in the life of Jesus. She has an utterly unique story, one that on some levels is hard to relate to. I haven't immaculately conceived a child, for instance. But she certainly was a normal peasant girl in a difficult, complicated situation that would threaten to overwhelm any of us. So, she has much to teach us as we look at her life. Perhaps that's what makes her ordinari-ness extraordinary. She welcomed the visitation. She allowed the unthinkable mystery to be part of her story. She bore the Son of God in her virginal womb.

Long Obedience

To be like Mary amid overwhelm is to have been faithful through-out our lives. When she meets Gabriel, she demonstrates a strong knowledge of the ways of God already, even at her young age. She

Mary, the Pierced One 151

grasps her nation's struggles, and she is not taken aback by what must've been a frightening encounter with an angel. And Mary is honest, asking the question of how this conception would happen. Hers was not a lack of faith; it was sheer curiosity. How, indeed, does one conceive without ever having sexual relations? Gabriel did not condemn her for asking the question; he simply answered it. When we are overwhelmed, we also can ask the Lord questions we have without fear of ridicule. The author of Hebrews states, "So let us come boldly to the throne of our gracious God. There we will receive his mercy, and we will find grace to help us when we need it most" (Hebrews 4:16). Overwhelm can result in two responses—we can endeavor to solve the problem on our own, trying to figure it out, or we can surrender and seek God as we question. Mary did the latter.

Knowing the Scriptures

Mary knew the Torah. She understood her nation's history and God's intersection of it. One observation many have made of late is that the church has a serious lack of biblical literacy. When we are overwhelmed, we tend to turn to gurus or social media or books, but we lack the skills to turn to the Word of God, where so much wisdom and help lies. You can't know the Bible without studying it for yourself. If your diet of the Scriptures comes once a week on a Sunday, you will not know the grand narrative as Mary did. We have a God who pursues his people—to the point of sending his Son to die in our place so we could live an abundant, kingdom-focused life.

Like Mary, we fit into that story. But we must study it to gain benefit from it—and not just the verses ripped out of context that sound soft and helpful-ish. I recently received a message on Instagram from someone taking my *90 Day Bible Reading*

152   The Most Overwhelmed Women of the Bible

Challenge who was upset at God as she read the Old Testament, calling him capricious. He is not capricious, but we only see that when we read the whole counsel of Scripture for ourselves. We see a holy God, an unholy people, and a persistent Redeemer bent on rescue. It's unfortunate that many of our evangelical spaces only emphasize the palatable parts of God (he loves you; he's for you; he wants you to be happy!) while neglecting the weightier aspects of him (he is completely other; he is jealous; he is a consuming fire). We've fallen prey to a false gospel that promises only prosperity. What happens when we run into inevitable pain and difficulties? This straw-man God we've believed in, who only exists for our consumption and benefit, falls down.

No, we need to know our Bibles. We need a robust theology of suffering, of knowing that we can have difficulties befall us like Job. We can read the Hall of Faith in Hebrews 11 and understand that we are made for more than this earth—that a kingdom perspective demands faith and a longer view. With an apt theology of suffering, where Jesus Himself suffered and died (so if we are His followers, we will inevitably suffer too), we are unsurprised by overwhelm. And, like Mary, we can ask God questions, remember his presence, and live *through* our pain rather than let pain derail us.

Trauma and Faith

Mary also persevered through what must've been deep trauma. In seeing her son crucified, she could have given up and walked away to nurse her very real wounds. But she was a disciple of her son, which is its own crazy thing to think about. (Would I follow my son as a guru, for instance?) Disciple-making meant that she followed in the footsteps of the other eleven disciples (Judas *did* walk away) who experienced the resurrection, knew about the ascension, and participated in waiting and praying for power from on high.

There have been so many times in my life when I've been tempted to give up. The trauma surrounding my early childhood felt like an impossible Everest to ascend. But footfall by footfall, with a lot of stumbling and tears, I'm learning the power of perseverance. Mary helps me to keep moving forward. There is much work to be done for the kingdom. But if the enemy of our souls can derail us through wayward relationships, painful circumstances, church hurt, elusive addiction, staggering poverty, or all-consuming fear (all forms of overwhelm), he wins a second victory. We must learn to reframe our pain and trials as opportunities. Jesus's brother James reminds us, "Dear brothers and sisters, when troubles of any kind come your way, consider it an opportunity for great joy" (James 1:2). And the Apostle Paul further states, "We can rejoice, too, when we run into problems and trials, for we know that they help us develop endurance" (Romans 5:3). In both scriptures, trials are seen as opportunities to rejoice—the opposite of how this world teaches us to behave when we're overwhelmed.

Continual Fellowship with God

Moment-by-moment connection to the Lord also helps us work through our overwhelming circumstances. In Mary's case, she moved to be near her son, and she followed him until his death. For us, it may look like the practice of Brother Lawrence, who found Jesus as he did menial tasks like washing the dishes. (For a very quick, inspirational read, pick up *The Practice of the Presence of God* by Brother Lawrence and you'll see this humble monk find the Lord throughout the mundane parts of his monastery life). Because we now have the Holy Spirit ever living within us, his presence is always available to us. It's a matter of stopping, being quiet (in our noisy culture), and simply communicating with him.

The Most Overwhelmed Women of the Bible

Today as I wrote this chapter, my conversation with God went like this: *Lord, I hear my husband talking to a client right now, but I know he's deeply weary of this job he has. We are so grateful for the provision, but would you please show us you see this situation? Would you give him the strength necessary to endure this workday? And, please, provide another job for him. He is weary, and I am weary on his behalf.* I also wrote out a prayer for him. As I write this book, I feel inadequate, so I ask Jesus to please give me insight as I write. This moment-to-moment communication keeps me close to him.

To be honest, I don't always constantly communicate with the Lord. It's far easier to run down rabbit trails of fear and entertain things that have yet to happen to us, fretting along the way. It takes discipline to turn to the Lord in every moment. And it takes humility, realizing we cannot do this life on our own. We need the Lord.

Truths About Healed You

- God often chooses the overlooked to do an overwhelming task.
- Studying the Word of God brings much profit to our souls.
- God promises to be with us even through the most difficult and bewildering of circumstances.
- To be a disciple is a daily, Holy Spirit–empowered act.
- Pentecost is available to all of us—because we have the Holy Spirit within us all the days of our lives.

Mary, the Pierced One

Questions for Discussion

1. How has your view of Mary changed after reading this chapter, if at all?
2. Why do you think we overlook Mary in our study of the gospels and Acts? What new thing did you realize about her lengthy story?
3. What kinds of emotions would you have felt if you were in Mary's position during the angelic visitation? The birth of Jesus? Fleeing to Egypt? The miracle in Cana? Watching your son suffer and die on the cross?
4. How, specifically, could Mary have been overwhelmed in each part of her story? What do you learn from her about how to navigate overwhelm?
5. What cultural changes have taken place since Mary's story? What has remained the same?

CHAPTER NINE

The Widow, the Broke One

She stood apart in the Temple, something she was accustomed to doing. A poor widow had little value in this world, she knew. But she needed to listen to the Teacher, because every time she heard his voice, she felt less alone, and, thankfully, as an unseen person, she could creep into places and remain anonymous. Jesus was the man's name whose beauty beckoned her closer. Some had rumored him to be a messiah, others a great prophet, while the religious leaders dismissed him altogether and seemed to make it their aim to discredit the one who gave sight to the blind, freedom to the captives, and health to the broken.

Today he seemed weary from their many questions. Almost exasperated. But she got the impression that he remained in the Temple courts on a mission, and that internal mission fueled his steady responses. He told of wicked farmers, and by the scowl on her leaders' faces, she knew he told the story against them, exposing

158 The Most Overwhelmed Women of the Bible

their hypocrisy. She steadied her breathing, kept to herself, and watched the drama unfold.

They pestered him about taxes, marriage puzzles about the resurrection, the most important commandment, and who the son of David was. He asked, "Since David himself called the Messiah 'my Lord,' how can the Messiah be his son?"

This made her laugh because the tongues of the religious scoffers were tied with that query. Jesus stood, motioning around him with a strong arm. She watched as his robes caught the light, as if God himself, may he be praised, shone down upon him. He gathered a crowd around himself, indicating he would teach. "Beware of these teachers of religious law! For they like to parade around in flowing robes and receive respectful greetings as they walk in the marketplaces. And how they love the seats of honor in the synagogues and the head table at banquets."

A murmur erupted from a passel of leaders to his left. Once again, this Jesus was teaching against them, exposing their pride. She could see hatred in their countenances, and she sighed. Jerusalem had become notorious for hating its prophets. Harming them, too.

Shaded in the corner, away from the gaze of many, she watched as Jesus gestured with his hands.

"Yet they shamelessly cheat widows out of their property and then pretend to be pious by making long prayers in public."

What?

This very thing had happened to her. How could the Teacher have known? She now lived in a tiny, borrowed room of another widow's home who had taken pity upon her. The leaders had told her the Lord needed her house—and who was she to argue with the Lord?—only to find out that they had profited from the sale of her home. She wanted to run to Jesus, throwing off all propriety, and embrace him, thanking him effusively for bringing her plight out

The Widow, the Broke One   159

into the open. But she remained where she was, rubbing two small coins together in her hands—the last lifeline for a meal.

"Because of this, they will be more severely punished," Jesus said.

But would they? She had seen the privilege of the ruling elite, and it seemed that they never got their comeuppance. Nevertheless, she could not spend her thoughts on this, as they were unfruitful. Instead, she prayed, *Dear God in heaven, thank you for seeing me and for bringing a ray of light to me today. Jesus's words make me feel that you see me, and that you will take care of me. I'm grateful. I love you. And please receive this tiny gift as my thanks for all you do for the widow, the orphan, the poor, the alien. We are privileged to be desolate because the desolate receive your specific, kindhearted consolation.*

The Teacher looked weary after this rebuke. He sat down near the place she planned to go, which both unnerved and excited her. The collection box was the designated spot for the people of God to tithe and bring offerings. For a long time, she didn't move from her shadowed corner, realizing such important people dropped in their offerings with pomp and pride. And they had much to be proud of. They dropped large sums of money into the box and seemed to be trying to get others to notice their generosity. One man dropped a large coin in, then looked around. He cleared his throat so others would notice, then proceeded to drop gold coin after gold coin. Each one clanked a chorus of wealth. Jesus, though, said nothing about the substantial gift. He didn't even look the man's way.

She fought within herself, wondering if she should place her pittance in the pot. But then she remembered the provision of God in the past. How he had multiplied her means much like the way he provided for the widow with a little cask of oil in the ancient stories. God deserved her all, her everything, and no amount of

160   The Most Overwhelmed Women of the Bible

embarrassment could hold her back from honoring him with all she had. So she rose from her shadowed place and slowly made her way toward the collection box. Her joints ached, her eyes burned under a relentless sun, and her feet felt sodden to the pavers. Still, she persisted, rubbing the mites together as if doing so would increase their fortune. No such magic happened, however.

Now standing at the Temple treasury box, she examined her two wee coins, amounting to a small percentage of a day's wage. So little, but all she had. They represented her last bit of wealth, the promise of a meager meal. "But God, you are worth it," she whispered. With no fanfare, she looked around, preferring anonymity—after all, the God of the secret place often rewarded those who did things in secrecy, where no one knew their sacrifice. While the other offerings had clanked, hers plinked. One coin. Two coins. She padded away, her stomach empty, but her heart full of the goodness of God.

She returned to her quiet, shaded corner, curious what else this Jesus would say.

Jesus looked her way, then nodded, as if he knew everything about her. He smiled.

She worried.

What would he say? Would he tell a story about the likes of her? Would she be a wicked farmer who stoned the prophets? Would she be the people with flowing robes and long public prayers? Nothing escaped this man's notice, she knew, as if he perceived the intentions of every person's heart, then lay it out bare before the Temple crowd.

"I tell you the truth," he told the men surrounding him by the treasury. "This poor widow has given more than all the others who are making contributions."

What? But what I gave was the smallest offering of them all. Surely, he cannot mean that.

"For they gave a tiny part of their surplus." He gestured toward the lingering crowd of people who had just given their offerings. "But she," he said, "poor as she is, has given everything she had to live on."

He is telling the truth. It was all I had. And now I have nothing. But this man of truth had given her a gift—the gift of acknowledgment, of seeing her, of honoring her gift. Though hungry, she felt such happiness well up in her that her hunger seemed a passing memory in light of joy's blossoming. He saw her. He noticed her. He appreciated her sacrifice.

The Temple seemed to glow that day as she watched the afternoon turn to dusk. The light of the sun highlighted the majesty of the ancient building, the place her people would sacrifice and meet with the Almighty.

She noticed Jesus leaving the treasury, and one of his disciples gesturing toward the Temple's magnificence. "Teacher," he said. "Look at these magnificent buildings! Look at the impressive stones in the walls."

She took note of them as well. This place she had come to treasure held all her wealth. And her heart.

"Yes," Jesus said, "look at these great buildings. But they will be completely demolished. Not one stone will be left on top of another!"

What could Jesus mean? This Temple was the bedrock, the foundation of her nation's spiritual life. How could such a horrible thing happen? But then she thought back over Israel's difficult history of idolatry and exile, of slavery and seas of deliverance, of widows like Naomi who turned bitter (then hope-filled) and queens like Esther who rescued her people from annihilation. Ebb and flow. Life and death. Captivity to freedom to captivity, then a remnant who returned. People changed. Empires were fickle. Temples fell.

162 The Most Overwhelmed Women of the Bible

But God, who made them all, always stood. He was who she worshiped today. He was the One she set her hope firmly upon. No stone could offer solace. No building could shelter her the way God had. No edifice provided for her in the quiet obscurity of her need. No, only God could be a shelter, a refuge.

Part of her wanted to follow Jesus and hear what he said of this Temple desecration, but another part of her felt the weight of the day, and her fatigue meant it was time to go home. As she took each step toward her little room that had become a haven in the past few years, she smiled because she knew that what little she had meant something, and that sacrifice for the sake of the God of Israel mattered.

Before she entered her home, she felt a hand upon her shoulder. She turned, but no one was there. But at her feet sat a basket of ripe figs—just enough to satisfy an evening hunger. With tears in her eyes, she threw her hands heavenward and thanked El Roi, the God Who Sees.

The Biblical Narrative

It's entirely important to look at the context of the widow's story found in Mark 12:41–44 and Luke 21:1–4. Both place her act of obedience after Jesus reprimanded (quite severely) the religious leaders and before a prediction of the Temple's demise. Why is that? Think about it: Her offerings, which represented all she had, were given for the upkeep of a Temple that would topple. If she did hear Jesus's words after her offering (as I have posited in the story above), how would she have felt?

Jesus's foretelling of the Temple's demise here was a foreshadowing of a new kingdom, a new way of doing religious life. No longer would the Temple be central to worship. We see this same shift in Jesus's words in John 4 when he meets the woman at the well. She puzzles over the different locales for worship—for Jews it is the Temple in Jerusalem, but for the Samaritans it's Mount Gerizim. Jesus responds, "Believe me, dear woman, the time is coming when it will no longer matter whether you worship the Father on this mountain or Jerusalem. . . . But the time is coming—indeed it is here now—when true worshippers will worship the Father in spirit and in truth. The Father is looking for those who will worship him that way" (John 4:21, 23). When the Upper Room's tongues of fire descended on the new church, followers of Jesus would *become* the Temple.

A cursory understanding of the structure of the Temple is important here. Earlier, Jesus was in the Court of Gentiles (outer area), turning over tables. Where the widow gives her coins is in the Court of the Women, which is closer to the inner court where all the sacrifices are made. So, in the narrative, we are moving closer and closer to the center of Jewish life. When Jesus watched the others "putting their gifts into the temple treasury," the Greek word here does not have the connotation of "put." The word is *ballo*, which looks a lot like ball, and it's indicative of the kind of action the people were performing. The word means to throw or cast. This verb is in the present tense, and it indicates a continual action. The receptacles in the treasury were, according to Precept Austin's commentary on Luke 2, "thirteen trumpet-shaped, metal receptacles (*shapharoth*), each marked with a Hebrew letter, stood in the court of the women to receive the gifts of the worshippers for the benefit of the Temple and for the Temple tax."[1] So they would make a noise when someone threw their coins in—think toll booths from years ago, where you had to cast your coins into a basket, and the tossing caused a clinking noise.

The word for poor here (Luke 21:2) is *penichros*, and it means someone who is wretchedly, completely poor. This is the only time the term is used in the New Testament.[2] In the other passage where this story is recounted (Mark 12:42), the word for poor is *ptochos*, which means to cower, cringe, crouch, or hide yourself— that's how poor the widow was, so destitute that she cowered. The *leptos*, or the coin she uses, is the only time this term is also used in the gospels. It connotes the peeling back of the bark of a tree, creating a thin sheet, so it means thinness or smallness. That she had two of these "thin" coins is instructive. She could have held one back, but she chose to give them both. Its value is one one-hundredth of a denarius, which was the common daily wage, so the total makes it 2/100th of a wage. In today's world, if a daily wage is $160.00 ($20.00 x 8 hours), what she donated was a little less than $4.00.

Dr. Darrel Bock of Dallas Theological Seminary further illustrates the significance of the widow's gift:

> Jesus's point is not so much to rebuke others' contributions as to exalt a contribution that otherwise would have been underappreciated. Sometimes little gifts cost a great deal more than big gifts do, and their merit is in the sacrifice they represent. In fact, real giving happens when one gives sacrificially. Interestingly, research has shown that when people's income increases their proportion of charitable contributions tends to drop. We tend to give less the more we are blessed. How would Jesus assess this trend?[3]

To answer Bock's question is to look at his effusive language about the widow's sacrifice. "This poor widow has given more than all the rest of them. For they have given a tiny part of their surplus, but she, poor as she is, has given everything she has" (Luke 1:3–4). His emphasis was not upon the actual monetary value, but on the

The Widow, the Broke One   165

spiritual value the sacrifice represented. Imagine if a rich person gave every last bit of wealth they had! Certainly, we would praise such a sacrifice. But when this poor widow does exactly the same thing, no fanfare came (except Jesus's sweet acknowledgment of her act). Earlier in Luke, we do see an exchange between Jesus and the rich young ruler, where Jesus does ask this very thing—to sell all a person has and give away that money to the poor, then to follow him. The man walked away sad because he loved his riches more than he wanted to follow Jesus (see Luke 18:18–27).

We also must remember Jesus's ability to read people's minds and know their hidden motives. One could give away everything yet have improper motives if they're doing it for status or recognition. But this widow, according to Jesus, had pure motives. Paul reminds us just how deeply the Lord knows our hearts and how prone we are to making rash judgments. Only God's judgments are correct. "So don't make judgments about anyone ahead of time—before the Lord returns. For he will bring our darkest secrets to light and will reveal our private motives. Then God will give to each one whatever praise is due" (1 Corinthians 4:5). This is what he did in the widow's case—he praised her.

Her giving did not warrant her salvation, however. Her actions didn't secure her eternity—they, instead, were a demonstration of an already changed heart. And that's where it's important for us to remind ourselves of the inside-out nature of the gospel. We do not superimpose rules from the outside to make a pious show (like the Pharisees, Scribes, Sadducees, and religious leaders). We experience a changed heart, then our actions naturally flow from that center. In James 2, we see a strong rebuke of those who give preferential treatment to the rich while treating the poor poorly. The author concludes the chapter with these pointed words: "Just as the body is dead without breath, so also faith is dead without good works" (James 2:26).

What Does This Mean for Overwhelmed You?

Economic Stress

Perhaps the greatest form of overwhelm we face is economic stress or insecurity. I know when I'm in that place, fear takes over, and I begin to act more like Mr. Scrooge than this dear widow. I hoard, shrinking inside myself, giving in to worry. Money occupies my waking thoughts. I find ways to finagle more or save what we have. Growing up in an economically precarious way influenced who I am today. I remember my grandmother, who lived through dire poverty in the south, constantly being haunted by that time in her life, so much so that she had a bunker-like storeroom in her basement full of expired cans, just in case. I must say, when my pantry is less than full, I beeline to the store to keep it restocked.

But this widow did the opposite of our entrenched fear nature. She gave it all away, based on her already close connection to the Lord and her ability to believe him to be her provider. The Apostle Paul talks about the power of this kind of sacrificial giving in 2 Corinthians 8:3–5: "For I can testify that they gave not only what they could afford, but far more. And they did it of their own free will. They begged us again and again for the privilege of sharing in the gift for the believers in Jerusalem. They even did more than we had hoped, for their first action was to *give themselves to the Lord* and to us, just as God wanted them to do" (emphasis mine). This kind of giving erupts from an already existing trust in the One who is trustworthy. When we surrender ourselves to the Lord (because we love him so much), it's no wonder that our connection to fleeting things like money loses its bite.

When we were struggling financially earlier in our marriage, we had an opportunity to test this idea of God being our provider.

We sold a car to a relative one time, and he made payments to us. One horrible day, he got into a life-altering accident and totaled the car, still owing us the car's value. We prayed about our response, asking God to reveal what we should do. In that instance, the Lord told us to forgive the debt and allow him to recoup the insurance to get a stronger start in life. The thrifty part of me (and as the one who paid the bills and knew what little we had) battled this decision initially. But we had been given so much by the Lord, and perhaps this could be a tangible demonstration of the gospel to our relative. So we did it. And let me tell you: joy erupted. To be able to relieve another's financial burden brought us so much joy. And God did provide for us. And he continues to do so.

When we near the end of our lives, I think we'll be more bothered by our times of fear-based miserliness. But we will not regret generosity. We will be grateful for those times we surrendered completely to the Lord. I have been both in this life—wildly generous and terribly fearful. But I'm grateful for those moments when my faith had feet, and I trusted God through a trying financial time. As I write this, we are facing another financial fear. I cannot fix it. But I am praying that the Lord will help me not revert to hoarding in the basement storeroom, and instead live open-handedly both toward the Lord and for those in need.

The widow teaches us that financial overwhelm is real. But that God sees it all. He knows our needs before we even voice them. And any sacrifice we give, he takes note of. God's heart is bent toward the quartet of the vulnerable: the widow, the orphan, the poor, and the foreigner. He loves to take care of them, but he often does that through us. Consider this indictment against Israel, who rejected these vulnerable people:

168   The Most Overwhelmed Women of the Bible

Then this message came to Zechariah from the Lord: "This is what the Lord of Heaven's Armies says: Judge fairly, and show mercy and kindness to one another. Do not oppress widows, orphans, foreigners, and the poor. And do not scheme against each other. Your ancestors refused to listen to this message. They stubbornly turned away and put their fingers in their ears to keep from hearing. They made their hearts as hard as stone, so they could not hear the instructions or the messages that the Lord of Heaven's Armies had sent them by his Spirit through the earlier prophets. That is why the Lord of Heaven's Armies was so angry with them." (Zechariah 7:8–12)

Hard Hearts

This exchange between Jesus and the religious leaders was an indictment of the latter's hard-heartedness. The widow served as a troubling contrast between the proud and the humble, the independent and the dependent, the stingy and the generous, the self-sufficient and the God-dependent. She serves as an example of wholehearted devotion, of exercising trust during overwhelming circumstances. To surrender is to trust. To relinquish our vice-grip on control is to remind ourselves that control is an illusion and that God is perfectly capable of being in control of our lives. He loves us. He sees us. He knows our needs. He loves to take note of us. And he is cheering us on when we demonstrate faithfulness through the power of the Spirit that lives within.

The widow gave her last bits of cash for the betterment of the Temple. We have been given the very presence of God in the Temple of our hearts. Our reaction to that beautiful gift is surrender, gratitude, and generosity.

When I think of hardened hearts, I remember Hosea 10:12: "I said, 'Plant the good seeds of righteousness, and you will harvest a crop of love. Plow up the hard ground of your hearts, for now is the time to seek the LORD, that he may come and shower righteousness upon you.'" To deal with a hardened heart is to do something—to plow, to work the soil of our clay-baked hearts. This is active, not passive. A longing, a yearning, a desire to be set free from bitterness and cynicism. This is a prayer the Lord loves to answer.

Other-ism

This poor widow was most likely advanced in years, and for this she was possibly overlooked. Her circumstances, certainly, were overwhelming. That Jesus noticed her is instructive. Whereas widows cannot contribute to the economic viability of a nation per se, they can be viewed as a drain. But more than that, especially in our culture today, we can simply let those older than us go without acknowledgment, as if they don't exist. In a culture of ageism, we've bought into the lie that the sole value of a soul is equated to what they do, provide, and work on. This widow is valuable. She performed a radically sacrificial act. Jesus brought attention to her.

In many churches today, we see a favoring of young leaders. While it's entirely important to raise them up, provide mentorship and guidance, and willingly welcome them into greater responsibility, we harm the body of Christ when we dismiss and dismantle the aged in our midst. They are the folks with deep wisdom, powerful experience, and profound faith.

But this problem is not merely for the older people in our midst. We can make someone "outside" or "other" by the way we categorize them. We can see people as in or out. When we forget that the whole body of Christ includes all sorts of ages and nationalities, we

The Most Overwhelmed Women of the Bible

lose sight of the beautiful diversity Jesus meant us to experience. God himself arranges his body as he wants it. "But our bodies have many parts, and God has put each part just where he wants it" Paul writes in 1 Corinthians 12:18.

How overwhelming it could be for someone who doesn't feel like they belong! What a burden to bear in our churches. Our task as Christ-followers is to let the anthem of Revelation 7:9 echo through us: "After this I saw a vast crowd, too great to count, from every nation and tribe and people and language, standing in front of the throne and before the Lamb. They were clothed in white robes and held palm branches in their hands." There is no "other" in the kingdom. All who bear the name of Christ belong. No one is expendable. No one is too young or too old. No nationality prevents us from experiencing the joy of fellowship with other believers.

Instead of overwhelming people by excluding them, we should be overwhelming them by welcoming them into our midst. This is the art of hospitality—the basis of which we clearly saw in the Book of Acts, where all believers from different backgrounds had everything in common and made sure to meet the needs of those less fortunate.

Truths About "Rich" You

- God knows your needs.
- How we treat the vulnerable in our midst matters.
- Surrender is a signpost of the kingdom.
- We are the Temple of God!
- God notices when you're faithful, even in quiet moments.

The Widow, the Broke One 171

Questions for Discussion

1. Why do you think the two gospel writers (Mark and Luke) included this story?
2. Have you read the widow's mite story in context before? What stood out to you in reading the passages and stories surrounding it?
3. How does the widow demonstrate faith?
4. How difficult would it have been for Jewish people to grasp that the Temple would eventually cease to be the center of their religious activity?
5. Recount a time when you had to fully rely on God for financial provision. What happened?

CHAPTER TEN

Priscilla, the Displaced One

"There are times I miss home," Priscilla told her husband, Aquila. She could smell the scent of the sea, an unfamiliar aroma—not unwelcomed.

"But, alas," Aquila said with a glint in his eye, "look where we are, dear one!" He gestured to their Mediterranean home nestled in the countryside near Corinth. "Has not the Lord blessed us with this and a stronger business?"

Tentmaking supplies scattered throughout their home-business, so much so that they had to step over pegs and supports to find their way to their living quarters. Priscilla nodded. "Rome did have its oppressions," she said, "thanks to Claudius."

Aquila took her hand. "God has brought us here for a special purpose; I know it. We will acclimate soon enough. Come, let's pray."

As the sun waned on the horizon and dusk settled in, together they asked God for favor, for new relationships, for purpose in their

174   The Most Overwhelmed Women of the Bible

relocation. When she said "Amen," Aquila's stomach grumbled. Priscilla laughed, setting about to make their evening meal—a simple supper of bread, figs, and greens.

A rapping at the outer door caught her attention. Who could that be at this time of night? She exchanged a glance with Aquila, whose eyes told her he would take care of this. When he opened the door, she saw a travel-weary man with piercing blue eyes.

"I am Paul," he said. "And I understand from the brothers and sisters nearby that we share the same trade." He pointed at the tent-making equipment dotting the inner courtyard.

"Come in," Aquila said. "Yes, we are tentmakers. You must be the same?"

Priscilla gathered the scraps from dinner and gave their visitor a plate of food. There was something about this man that stirred her—a knowing that they shared the same heart for the Good News.

And that is precisely what played out well into the night. They recounted their stories while Paul told of his miraculous conversion on the road to Damascus, and they shared their testimonies—hers as a Roman citizen finding Christ, and her husband as a Jew meeting him as well—and how the Lord brought them both together to further his kingdom. They, like Paul, funded their work for Christ through the sweat of their brows as they crafted tents for the locals.

As the stars pinpricked the sky that night, they had formed an alliance—both of trade and of heart. They would be purveyors of the gospel together in this new locale.

Paul peppered his conversation with theology, the gospel, and church governance as they labored side by side in the tentmaking business. It was as if his words completed a picture she and

Priscilla, the Displaced One   175

Aquila saw, though blurry, and now Paul's experiences and study refocused the picture. The clearer it became, the more enflamed her heart grew for sharing the message of Jesus Christ with everyone she saw.

Alongside Paul and Aquila, they entered synagogues in the area, hoping to persuade Jews (and even Greeks!) to augment their view of Jesus the Messiah. Priscilla watched as Paul demonstrated from the Torah how Jesus was the Suffering Servant meant to rescue both Jews and Gentiles from their sins. Their fellowship only increased with the inclusion of Silas and Timothy, who joined them from Macedonia. On one Sabbath, she felt Paul's arguments to be entirely persuasive only to watch as someone insulted Paul, calling him blasphemous names, and yelling their opposition. Paul took the abuse for a long period of time, but he eventually stepped away from the crowd hurling insults and said in a firm voice, "Your blood is upon your own heads—I am innocent. From now on I will go preach to the Gentiles." He rubbed his sandals in the dirt outside the threshold of the synagogue, then shook the dust from his feet.

It was then that Paul left their home (he had stayed there quite some time) and stayed with Titius Justus, who happened to be a Gentile located (surprisingly!) right next door to another synagogue. But soon, its leader Crispus bent the knee to Jesus, including his entire household. Oh, how they had rejoiced on that day! It seemed like believers kept multiplying, both Jew and Gentile, and she had the privilege to witness many baptisms. Their days were full of work by light and ministry by dark. And she spent her time studying when she could to be able to correctly handle the word of truth.

"Aquila, Priscilla," Paul called one evening from the exterior of their compound. "Come, please."

They rushed out, Priscilla fearing what he might say. They'd grown accustomed to caution, threats, and possible retribution.

176   The Most Overwhelmed Women of the Bible

Persecution had woven itself into the fabric of their lives, tightly bound like the canvas used to make tents.

"What is it?" Aquila asked. He invited Paul back into their home, then lit a torch to illuminate the night.

"I had a vision," he told them. "And it is encouraging." He explained how the Lord spoke directly to him.

"What did the Lord tell you?" she asked.

Paul smiled. "Not to be afraid and to speak out, to not be silent. He said, 'For I am with you, and no one will attack and harm you, for many people in this city belong to me.'"

"That *is* good news," Priscilla said. "And I have seen God continue to add to our numbers. Does this mean you will stay?"

"Indeed, it does," Paul said.

They celebrated by thanking God, singing a hymn, and sharing a late-night meal together.

The days were long, and the stress kept building in Priscilla's heart. The same unease that had pelted her when Claudius governed Rome returned when Gallio was appointed as governor of Achaia. "His appointment is fueling the Jews' distrust," she told Aquila one evening. "It will not go well for us." She looked around at their business, all they had built for themselves and the kingdom, and felt that familiar pang—God was stirring their nest, making their lives uncomfortable to move them on to other kingdom endeavors.

The next day, the foreboding she felt materialized when some angry Jewish leaders seized their friend Paul. She, along with Aquila, followed along to the governor's residence, worry growing with every step she took along the cobbled streets. Shouting arose as she neared the governor's residence. A voice, one she couldn't place but that had the same sound of many who opposed them, said, "This man is persuading people to worship God in ways that are contrary to our law!" A cry rose from the crowd.

Priscilla prayed. *Please grant Paul favor.*

She drew closer to the commotion and saw Paul stand amid the crowd. He cleared his throat, which she knew meant he was ready to make a defense. She kept praying.

But, to her surprise, Gallio stepped in front of Paul. "Listen, you Jews," he said. "If this were a case involving some wrongdoing or serious crime, I would have a reason to accept your case. But since it is merely a question of words and names and your Jewish law, take care of it yourselves. I refuse to judge such matters." He dismissed them all. And in the strange fickleness of crowds, those who brought the accusations turned on their own—a man named Sosthenes, a synagogue leader, whom they beat and bloodied.

Gallio watched but did nothing.

After that, they continued sharing the Good News often, making tents to provide for themselves, and praying often about what the Lord would want them to do next. Paul made his way to Cenchrea nearby to fulfill a vow (dear Aquila took on the task of shaving Paul's head). After that, Paul invited them to join him in Syria.

Priscilla knew this day would come—when they would leave another place they had called home, uprooting themselves and following the Way wherever it took them. The irony of their trade was not lost on her—those who made tents were bound to be nomadic, after all.

They ported in Ephesus, then followed their typical pattern of reasoning with Jewish people in the local synagogue. So many responded well that they asked Paul to stay. Priscilla wished for this as well. A year and a half with Paul in Corinth had been the best discipleship journey, and she felt unready for ministry on her own

178   The Most Overwhelmed Women of the Bible

with Aquila. Still, she trusted God to take care of them. Paul told them both, "I will come back later, God willing." The day he set sail, she hid her tears in her *palla*, telling herself all would be well.

She spent much time reestablishing herself in Ephesus with Aquila, finding camaraderie in the local believers and building into each one that the Lord brought her way. Overwhelm threatened her, what with a new culture, a new way of doing things, and a life without their dear friend Paul. Priscilla prayed again that the Lord would show them just what he had for them. And he answered—in a surprising way.

She and Aquila heard the mighty Apollos teach in the synagogue. His reputation came by way of Alexandria in Egypt. The man knew the Scriptures, and his teaching was powerful and eloquent. He spoke of Jesus with such passion, talking of the life of Jesus with stunning accuracy. She thrilled at his words.

"And the baptism of John," Apollos said, "is a baptism we must follow, of repentance and forgiveness of sins."

He doesn't know the rest of the story!

As soon as Apollos finished teaching, Aquila invited Apollos to their home, and they gathered for a meal. From the beginning of John the Baptist's ministry to his beheading, to the miracles of Jesus, his supernatural provisions, healing all kinds of diseases, teaching about love and forgiveness and being blessed if you're poor in spirit, of the disciples who followed him to the end, the raising of Lazarus, and his power of the demonic—they explained the entire story to Apollos.

"The leaders of Israel were looking for a Messiah to vanquish Rome," Priscilla said. "But Jesus defied their expectations. Instead the very leaders who were supposed to honor Jesus chose to crucify him."

"No!" Apollos stood, alarm on his face. "It cannot be!"

"He had to suffer and die for us all," Aquila said.

Apollos sat, shaking his head. Then he put his face in his hands and wept.

Aquila placed a hand on his shoulder, then pointed to the darkening sky. "It is said that the sky was as dark as this at three in the afternoon, as if the earth was mourning."

"What else do I not know?" Apollos asked.

And that's when Priscilla smiled. "The best part of the truest story ever told. The grave could not hold our Lord, could not prevail against him. On Sunday, the third day, Jesus came out of the grave—gloriously alive!"

Apollos shouted. "What? He did?"

"Yes, and our friend Paul, who recently left here, witnessed him much, much later as he trekked toward Damascus," Aquila said. "Jesus is not dead. He is alive!"

"All praise to God," Apollos said. "Jesus is the Messiah indeed."

The church in Ephesus that met in their home sent Apollos on his way to Achaia, along with a letter explaining who he was and that he was trustworthy and would be of great benefit to the church there. It seemed to Priscilla that this life of faith often meant transition, hellos and goodbyes, and being willing to uproot for the cause of Christ.

Once Claudius died, they once again uprooted their livelihood and spent time in Rome, which no longer felt like home. Still, they were able to resume tentmaking operations and start a church where they lived. While there, she missed her friend Paul, who had become so

180 The Most Overwhelmed Women of the Bible

dear to them both. One day, she heard a knock at the outer court doorway and cautiously looked through the slats to see who it was. Life had become far more complicated there, knowing there were spies and persecutions and general mayhem. But a woman stood before her, and her face registered the kindness of God.

"Come in," she told the woman, ushering her into the compound. "I am Priscilla, and my husband Aquila and I live here. How can I help you?"

"I am Phoebe," she said. "I come from Paul in Cenchrea with a letter for your church."

Priscilla embraced her. "You are welcome, Phoebe. You must have had a very long journey."

The woman laughed. "It was full of adventure, I must admit."

After having a meal together, Phoebe spoke to their gathered community. She pulled out the scroll she had spirited through a long hike, a few boat trips, and another trek along the Appian way. Priscilla held her breath as Phoebe began to read the letter, deep into the night. When Phoebe neared the end, she looked at Priscilla, then read, "Give my greetings to Priscilla and Aquila, my co-workers in the ministry of Christ Jesus. In fact, they once risked their lives for me. I am thankful to them, and so are all the Gentile churches. Also give my greetings to the church that meets in their home." She continued reading greetings to many people in their fellowship, but Priscilla rested in those few sentences of commendation.

Though the work was lonely at times and full of unpredictability and upheaval, it was the friendship they shared with Paul that kept them joyful—that, and their communion with Jesus Christ, the one they owed their very lives to that empowered them both to uproot and replant. Perhaps they would return to Ephesus or Corinth soon. She did not know that future, but Priscilla marveled at all the Lord had done through them both.

The Biblical Narrative

We find the story of Priscilla (also known as Prisca) and her husband, Aquila, in Acts 18, 1 Corinthians 16, 2 Timothy 4, and Romans 16. Her name is now Hebrew in origin, but in the Latin, it meant *ancient*. Of the six times she is mentioned, her name is stated first most of those instances. Various opinions by scholars account for why this is. Perhaps she was more educated than Aquila, or she belonged to a different or greater societal class. Others have speculated she was more spiritually mature, but we really cannot know the actual reason.

The story unfolds in Corinth because Claudius, who ruled from 41–54 BCE, demanded that all Jews leave the capital city of Rome. It's estimated that there were about twenty thousand Jews living in or near Rome at the time, according to Precept Austin's commentary on Acts 18.[1] When it says Paul "*became acquainted* with a Jew named Aquila, born in Pontus, who had recently arrived from Italy with his wife, Priscilla" (Acts 18:2, emphasis mine), the verb there is the common Greek word *proserchomai*, which means to approach, come near, draw near, or visit.[2] When we look back on the book of 1 Corinthians, we see that Paul may have sought fellowship because of the stress he was under. "I came to you in weakness—timid and trembling" (1 Corinthians 2:3). What's interesting about Paul seeking out this couple was that it broke with his typical pattern of going to the synagogue in a village first. Perhaps his own overwhelm compelled him to find the couple.

Priscilla and Aquila's profession of tentmaking is mentioned only one time in the New Testament, but entire missionary movements (of bi-vocational ministry) have used this terminology as people sought to make disciples as a part of their regular workaday life. The word used is *skenopoios* (literally tent + make). While some tents were made from rough goat's hair, many at that time were made from leather (because of its ability to deflect rain).

The Most Overwhelmed Women of the Bible

Paul enjoyed a flourishing time in Corinth—he spent a year and a half there, reasoning with others and discipling Priscilla and Aquila. In fact, their relationship was so central to Paul's life that they became not merely co-laborers on tents, but they also brought the gospel to the world. Paul was particular about who he invited on missionary voyages (in Acts 15:36–41, he chose not to invite John Mark, for instance), so his welcoming of this couple speaks volumes about their integrity, ministry-mindedness, and fitness for the difficult work of church-planting.

While Paul continued his missionary endeavors, Priscilla and Aquila stopped at Ephesus (as they were on their way to Syria, initially), and ended up staying. Scripture is silent as to why, though Paul may have entrusted them with building up the believers there. The most critical part of their ministry involved an encounter in Ephesus with Apollos, a Jewish man from Alexandria (Egypt), which, at that time, was a part of the Roman Empire and its second largest city. He most likely came from the Jewish sector of Alexandria. According to the passage in Acts, he was eloquent and persuasive, but he only had a part of the gospel. Imagine hearing only the words of John the Baptist, who foretold of an imminent coming Messiah and the importance of preparing one's heart for that savior through repentance and baptism. He did know of Jesus, but he did not hear the remainder of the story—only that John had baptized Jesus.

Into this scenario stepped Priscilla and Aquila, who had been taught by Paul so well that they had the privilege of sharing the rest of the story with Apollos. Imagine how exciting that must have been for the Alexandrian Jew. He already believed in Jesus, but now he had the fullest picture of his sacrifice and resurrection. Here we see the kingdom math of multiplication demonstrated powerfully. Paul poured into this couple; they poured into Apollos; then, Apollos went as a missionary to Achaia, where he "proved to be of great

Priscilla, the Displaced One — 183

benefit to those who, by God's grace, had believed. He refuted the Jews with powerful arguments in public debate. Using the Scriptures, he explained to them that Jesus was the Messiah" (Acts 18:27b–28).

Not only that, but Priscilla and Aquila thwarted incomplete teaching. Because of Apollos's oratory skills, he could have spread a partial gospel throughout the region. But now because of the correction of his new friends, his gifts of persuasion could be used to preach the actual, full gospel to many.

Though Paul does not explicitly say how Priscilla and Aquila risked their lives for him (see Romans 16:4), they did demonstrate their fearless and fervent dedication to the Lord and their deep friendship with Paul. No doubt this risking provided much overwhelm in the moment.

What we know about Priscilla is this: She was faithful to bloom wherever she found herself. Whether at home or in foreign cities throughout the empire, she and Aquila sacrificed themselves, opening their home as a church wherever they traveled. As a church-planter myself, I deeply understand the sacrifice this kind of gospel lifestyle demands.

Later, when Paul writes to Timothy in prison, he fondly greets his friends. "Give my greetings to Priscilla and Aquila," Paul writes in 2 Timothy 4:19. They became partners in the gospel with the venerable apostle, but they were also close friends.

What Does This Mean for Overwhelmed You?

Aliens on Earth

There is so much to glean from the life of Priscilla. As a Roman exile, she knew the sting of not quite feeling at home wherever she traveled, which parallels our roles as aliens on this earth. The Apostle Peter wrote of this condition when he penned, "Dear friends, I warn you as 'temporary residents and foreigners' to keep away from worldly desires that wage war against your very souls. Be careful to live properly among your unbelieving neighbors. Then even if they accuse you of doing wrong, they will see your honorable behavior, and they will give honor to God when he judges the world" (2 Peter 2:11–12). As a tentmaker, she would have lived among people who were not her own, and she would've interacted with a wide variety of people.

Her life, vocation, and service all flowed together as service toward others. No doubt this would have been overwhelming. Do you ever feel like you wear too many hats? I do, constantly. But she somehow managed to keep ministry at the top of her priority list, perhaps seeing her vocation as simply a means to an end. And she flourished even while being nomadic. Of course, no one knows for sure how she felt about this kind of existence, but that Paul commends both her and Aquila means that he had respect for the way they lived their lives.

Perhaps you're not in the middle of a physical move, but your life feels like it's in upheaval. That is its own overwhelm. Finding Jesus amid the cacophony of voices, the endless to-do lists, or the uncertainty of the future is the key to learning to be more like Priscilla. May we all flower where we're seeded.

The Importance of Community

What I pull away from her life is simple, yet profound. Priscilla embraced deep community, particularly with the Apostle Paul. She opened her home to him, which gave her a unique opportunity to understand the gospel, learn theology, and hear about the nuanced needs of an ever-expanding church. Imagine all she learned about governance, elders, deacons, polity, dealing with conflict, and how to clearly communicate the gospel, not to mention the deep importance of discipleship. This she didn't learn through study, but by community experience. She would not be celebrated in the Bible had she and her husband not welcomed Paul into their home.

Relationships form us. We grow through iron-sharpening-iron friendships (see Proverbs 27:17). In fact, none of us grows in isolation. We need each other. And when life bends toward the overwhelming, we require community even more than before. Sadly, many of us experienced the opposite of this during the COVID-19 pandemic. Because of restrictions, our face-to-face conversations were replaced by Zoom calls—which furthered those feelings of isolation. I remember our daughter coming over to our house just for a hug because the loneliness of singleness in her house had messed with her mental health. Truth: We need each other. Proverbs 18:1 cautions, "Whoever isolates himself seeks his own desire; he breaks out against all sound judgment" (ESV).

We have friends who emulate Priscilla and Aquila—Nicole and Vincent, who live among the poor near the French Riviera. They modeled what a strong marriage is to children from broken, sometimes abusive homes. They open their home to some children who don't have a safe place to land. They tutor kids toward success in school, inviting the community to join them. They truly believe that making disciples is a long decision—it takes time and incarnational work. They remind me of the admonition, "We loved you so much that we shared with you not only God's Good News but our own lives too" (1 Thessalonians 2:8). To be honest, they're my heroes, my Priscilla and Aquila. They represent Jesus to me.

When Community Sours

More than any other cure for overwhelm, community is the best cure. But it's also the worst purveyor of pain. As I write this, I am struggling to reengage in community because what had been a

186 The Most Overwhelmed Women of the Bible

beautiful place of service, training, and fellowship for well over two decades (our former church) became a toxic place for us. And now we're putting our toes into a new church home, quite tentatively because of past pain. If that's you, I wish I could reach through these pages and give you a hug. There's no pain quite like the pain of church hurt. I've had to test the words I've preached to others: If you're wounded in negative community, you'll be healed in good community. The problem is, that's not so easy to do, particularly when the overwhelm comes under the steeple of a church, a place that is supposed to be a haven.

Priscilla is my heroine as I think about my life right now, how tentative I am to step back in, yet how willing she seemed to be to move on and make a home wherever she was. She also demonstrated slow obedience and the unseen qualities of discipleship. In a world of big ministries and big numbers, she spent her time with one: the Apostle Paul, who imparted his life in her and Aquila's lives. And then she poured into Apollos, who then reached many. When we are overwhelmed in thinking about our impact on this earth, we can get tripped up by whether we're making a splash. But God only calls us to simple obedience.

One step at a time.

One relationship at a time.

One conversation at a time.

Perhaps the bravest thing you'll do today is simply open up to a new, safe friend in the aftermath of being hurt.

A note about church hurt: Going back to church may stress you out or cause you to panic. That's a normal response to a traumatic event. Be gentle with yourself. If it's too overwhelming to sit in a pew, give yourself space and time to heal. Enter into safe relationships cautiously, pulling back if you feel unsafe. It may take time to heal, and that's okay.

Obedience Anyway

We may not discern the end of a small story we're in. We may be in the middle of an unfinished story, curious about the ending. We may have given a hug to a stranger twenty-three years ago, and unbeknownst to us, God used that kindness to bring about a revolution in that person's life. As disciples, God asks us to give without knowing the outcome. We are constantly part of a divine story that we won't see "the end" of until we get to the other side. That excites me, honestly. Knowing this life is an adventure in discipleship (in small ways and big) makes me realize the importance of simple, day-by-day obedience.

I don't think Priscilla grasped the dent she made in the kingdom in the daily work of tent-making and disciple-making, but history reveals her impact. Similarly, we may not know how much our small acts of obedience have changed the kingdom landscape. Still, we press on—even in the middle of overwhelm. Little by little.

When you grow discouraged about the "little" you are doing or the nebulousness of your current situation that has no satisfactory ending, take a gander down memory lane. Remember those times of bewilderment when you had no idea what God was doing, only to later understand his ways in retrospect. He is faithful. He knows your feelings of overwhelm, and he knows how to rescue you today. The story may end differently than you anticipated, but it will be good. He who begins good things will bring them to completion (see Philippians 1:6.)

Truths About Settled You

- Community is where you will grow.
- No matter where you live or where God moves you, you can flourish there.

188   The Most Overwhelmed Women of the Bible

- Bi-vocational ministry is valid and the way most people spread the gospel in the first century.
- We need to be ready in season and out of season to train the people who come into our lives.
- We may not know the outcome of our obedience, but we must obey anyway.

Questions for Discussion

1. How has your view of Priscilla changed after reading this chapter?
2. How does Priscilla's story during her many relocations encourage you when you face transition?
3. Who in your life are you discipling? Who is or has been discipling you?
4. Looking back, how has a small act of obedience flourished into fruit?
5. How does the collaborative ministry of Paul, Priscilla, and Aquila inform the way you do ministry today?

CONCLUSION

Overwhelmed No More

Perhaps you've picked up this book because you wanted to learn more about women in the Bible. Or maybe your book club has chosen this book for you, and you're obliging them. Or maybe it's the word *overwhelm* that has drawn you. My hunch is the latter. All of us battle overwhelm. All of us wear too many hats. All of us feel the weight of too much, too soon, too many.

But there is hope.

There is always hope.

And that hope comes from the pages of the Word of God, and it is fleshed out in our relationships. Considering that, would you mind if I prayed a blessing over you as you leave these pages?

When you feel overwhelmed:

May the Lord bring you comfort in the form of a friend.
May you find a place of quiet rest in the middle of life's mayhem.
May God encourage you specifically from his Word.

The Most Overwhelmed Women of the Bible

May you find solace in hidden obedience.
May you know your work matters for the kingdom.
May you encounter the living God in your weakness and fear.
May you hear "This is the way, walk in it."
May discouragement become a place to trust God's hand.
May God surprise you with his tangible nearness.
May you let go of that which easily entangles your mind.
May you seek the Lord with all your heart,
soul, mind, and strength.
May you gain insight into the ways of God.
May your worries, stressors, and fears seem small
in light of your great, big God.
May the voice of the enemy be silenced and
the whisper of God be alive.
May you know the Lord as your provider.
May your worth be settled simply because you are loved.
And may you go forth with joy.
Amen.

Acknowledgments

Thank you to the team at Skyhorse Publishing who championed this book and welcomed its inauguration. Thank you, Kathryn Riggs, for making the manuscript sing. I appreciate you, dear agent Joy Eggerichs Reed, for your kindness and compassion toward me—always. You believed the best about me, and for that I am grateful.

My prayer team, the Writing Prayer Circle, prays me through every manuscript. Gratitude goes to Jenny, Amy, Avril, Melissa, Kathy, Tabea, Roblee, Sabrina, Susan, Misty, Rebecca C., Patti, Cheryl, Misti, Aldyth, Ally, Amy, Elaine, Dusty, Paula, Kendra, Boz, Cristin, Yanci, Paul, Brandilyn, Richard, Sue, Christy, Alice, Susie, TJ, Dorian, Darren and Holly, Colette, Patricia, Cheri, Gina, Jessica, Michelle, Denise, Ellen, Lacy, Rebecca J., Lisa, Heidi, Becky, Lea Ann, Michelle W., Julie, Kristin, Becky, Sabina, Anna, Leslie, Tosca, Sophie, Diane, Nicole, Jody, Tim, Susan W., Sandi, Cheryl, Randy, Patrick, Holly, Cyndi, Katy O., Katy G., Judy M., Erin, Jeanne, D'Ann, Liz, Caroline, Anita, Ralph, and Hope. I truly believe all kingdom success of my books rests on your praying prowess.

Thank you to my new family at Redeemer Rockwall. You restored my hope in the church, and you didn't shun me for my own overwhelming wound. You have been the hands and feet of Jesus to me.

Jesus, thank you that during my own overwhelm, you brought me to a quiet place, ushered in people who encouraged me to rest, and reminded me that I am not the sum of my work or circumstances.

Notes

Introduction: Overwhelm as Oxygen

1 See also "Overwhelm, Underwhelm, Whelm," Grammarphobia, November 5, 2014, https://www.grammarphobia.com/blog/2014/11/whelm.html#:~:text=Oxford%20raises%20the%20possibility%20that,means%20to%20submerge%20or%20overwhelm.

2 "Overwhelm," Bible Hub, https://biblehub.com/topical/o/overwhelm.htm.

3 "John 1:5 Commentary," Precept Austin, updated June 6, 2024, https://www.preceptaustin.org/john_15_commentary#:~:text=NLT%20The%20light%20shines%20in,darkness%20did%20not%20overwhelm%20it.

Chapter One: Sarai, the Disbelieving One

1 That quote is mentioned here, among many other places: Leftbehind.com, "Left Behind.com Interview with Randy Alcorn About Heaven," Eternal Perspectives Ministries, March 30, 2010, https://www.epm.org/resources/2010/Mar/30/left-behindcom-interview-randy-alcorn-about-heaven/.

2   Mary DeMuth, "Delight Yourself in the Lord: What the Bible Teaches + 7 Tips," Logos, August 31, 2023, https://www.logos .com/grow/nook-delight-yourself-in-the-lord/.

Chapter Two: Zipporah, the Nomadic One

1   "Zipporah Meaning," Abarim Publications, last updated January 16, 2025, https://www.abarim-publications.com /Meaning/Zipporah.html.

2   Oswald Chambers, *My Utmost for His Highest* (Westwood: Barbour and Company, Inc., 1935), 11.

Chapter Three: Manoah's Wife, the Grieved One

1   Charles Haddon Spurgeon, "A Precious Drop of Honey," The Spurgeon Center, May 31, 1863, https://www.spurgeon .org/resource-library/sermons/a-precious-drop-of -honey/#flipbook/.

2   "Judges 13 Commentary" Precept Austin, last updated November 11, 2022, https://www.preceptaustin.org /judges_13_commentary.

Chapter Four: Naaman's Slave Girl, the Imprisoned One

1   "What Is Modern Slavery?" AntiSlavery.org, https://www .antislavery.org/slavery-today/modern-slavery.

2   Ibid.

Chapter Five: Huldah, the Burdened One

1 Tamar Kadari, "Huldah, the Prophet: Midrash and Aggadah," *Shalvi/Hyman Encyclopedia of Jewish Women*, Jewish Women's Archive, February 27, 2009, https://jwa.org/encyclopedia/article/huldah-prophet-midrash-and-aggadah.

2 John DelHousaye, "Who Are the Women Prophets in the Bible?" CBE International, June 5, 2009, https://www.cbeinternational.org/resource/q-who-are-women-prophets-bible.

3 John Gray, *I and II Kings: A Commentary* (Philadelphia: Westminster Press, 1963), 660.

4 "The Ordination of Women Deacons According to the Apostolic Constitutions," Wijngaards Institute for Catholic Research, https://www.womendeacons.org/rite-ordination-women-deacons-apostolic-constitutions/.

5 John Knox, *Works of John Knox*, 4th ed., vol. 4 (Eugene: Wipf & Stock Publishers, 2004), 357.

Chapter Six: Esther, the Fearful One

1 Charles Haddon Spurgeon, *A Good Start: A Book for Young Men and Women* (Abbotsford: Aneko Press, 2023). See also Charles Haddon Spurgeon, "Providence as Seen in the Book of Esther," The Spurgeon Center, November 2, 1874, https://www.spurgeon.org/resource-library/sermons/providence-as-seen-in-the-book-of-esther-2/#flipbook/.

2 "Esther 1-2 Commentary," Precept Austin, last updated January 18, 2025, https://www.preceptaustin.org/esther_1-2_commentary.

3 I am indebted to Michael G. Wechsler's article "Shadow and Fulfillment in the Book of Esther" in the *Bibliotheca Sacra*, BSAC 154:615, July 1997, https://www.galaxie.com/article/bsac154-615-02.

Chapter Seven: Elizabeth, the Barren One

1   Philip W. Comfort, *The Life Application New Testament Commentary* (Carol Stream: Tyndale House Publishers, 2001), 240–41, https://books.google.com/books?id=UpKsAwAAQBAJ&printsec=frontcover&source=gbs_ge_summary_r&cad=0#v=onepage&q&f=false.

2   Ibid.

3   Ibid.

4   "Luke 1 Commentary," Precept Austin, last updated December 18, 2024, https://www.preceptaustin.org/luke-1-commentary.

5   "Luke 1," The NET Bible, https://netbible.org/bible/Luke+1.

Chapter Eight: Mary, the Pierced One

1   Kelley Mathews, "Mary, the Mother of Jesus: The First and Longest Disciple," *Seminary Now Blog*, March 16, 2023, https://seminarynow.com/pages/blog?p=mary-the-mother-of-jesus&ampDeviceId=e56eaf7f-c8b4-4aeb-b7a0-ccbe059339ae&ampSessionId=1737676800040.

2   Dr. Ian Paul, "The Annunciation to Mary in Luke 1," Psephizo.com, December 18, 2020, https://www.psephizo.com/biblical-studies/the-annunciation-to-mary-in-luke-1/.

3   Mathews, "Mary, the Mother of Jesus."

Chapter Nine: The Widow, the Broke One

1   "Luke 21 Commentary," Precept Austin, last updated March 17, 2024, https://www.preceptaustin.org/luke-21-commentary.

2   Ibid.

3   Ibid.

Notes 197

Chapter Ten: Priscilla, the Displaced One

1 "Acts 18 Commentary," Precept Austin, last updated February 12, 2024, https://www.preceptaustin.org/acts-18-commentary.

2 Ibid.